Liszt

Anthony Wilkinson

The Musicians

General Editor: Geoffrey Hindley

M

To my parents

SBN 333 15064 3

First published 1975 by
Macmillan London Limited
London and Basingstoke
Associated companies in New York, Dublin,
Melbourne, Johannesburg and Delhi

Picture research by Ann Davies
Music copying by Mary Criswick

Filmset by BAS Printers Limited,
Over Wallop, Hampshire
Printed in Great Britain by Waterlow (Dunstable) Ltd.

Contents

Chapter 1

The Prodigy

In the year of the 'Great Comet', 1811, an earthly star was born: to Adam and Anna List, in the Hungarian village of Raiding, on Friday, 22 October, a son, Ferencz. So brightly did the comet burn that night that the local Gypsies took it to be an omen of good fortune, and foretold a dazzling future for the newborn child. So frequently was this story told that the boy became invested with a sense of destiny that was itself destined to shape his future.

Franz Liszt—the 'z' being added later to avoid the Magyar pronunciation 'Lischt'—grew up a delicate child. During her pregnancy Anna had fallen down a disused well shaft and was only rescued after several hours. Wet, bruised, and frozen to the marrow she suffered severe shock. Though the birth was unexpectedly without complications, the child was sickly and weak, subject to nervous attacks, and was stricken once with a cataleptic seizure so severe that he was thought to be dead.

An only child, overprotected by anxious parents, Franz developed slowly in all respects other than music. His musical gifts originated in his father, and were developed under his guidance. Adam Liszt's recent promotion, in 1809, from clerk to land steward on the Esterhazy estates had meant a move for his family from the immediate vicinity of the palace at Kismarton to the land steward's tied house at the isolated peasant community of Raiding. Their unassuming family home is still the most important house in the tiny village.

It was a high price to pay for a modest rise in salary, for Adam was a gifted musician who had flourished in the Esterhazy court, with its brilliant musical tradition that gloried in the names of Mozart and Haydn. He could perform on most of the instruments of the orchestra, though he was thought most proficient on the violin, cello, guitar and piano. He played in the orchestra at Kismarton and even composed

Left: Liszt as a young boy
Below: Anna List, his mother and Adam List, his father

a *Te Deum*, which he dedicated to the Prince Nicholas. He was a good friend and card-playing companion of Mozart's most gifted pupil, Hummel.

Though temporarily deprived, his musical enthusiasms were in the course of time to be more richly rewarded than he could ever have expected. In a letter to Prince Esterhazy he recounted the first indication he had had of his son's talent:

At the age of six, he heard me play Ries' *Concerto in C Minor*. Franz, bending over the piano, listened absorbed. In the evening, coming in from a short walk in the garden, he sang the theme of the concerto. We made him sing it again. He did not know what he was singing.

At about this time the boy began to improvise instinctively upon the piano, before he had learned to read notation. Recognizing his natural gifts, Adam began in earnest with daily lessons, and progress was so spectacular that in less than two years we find him petitioning the Prince to be transferred, for the sake of his son's musical education, to Vienna:

The fact that within twenty-two months he has easily overcome any difficulty in the works of Bach, Mozart, Beethoven, Clementi, Hummel, Cramer, etc., and can play the hardest piano pieces at sight, in strict tempo, correctly and without any mistakes, represents in my opinion giant progress.

In October 1820, at the age of nine, Franz played before an audience for the first time in the Old Casino in Sopron, where he shared the programme with the blind flautist-pianist, Baron von Braun. The reception was so encouraging that a further concert was arranged for the child, alone, at Pozsony (now Bratislava), at which he caused a sensation with his performance of Ries' difficult concerto and with his improvisations on well-known

themes. The *Pressburger Zeitung* carried his first review:

Last Sunday, on the 26th [November], at noon, the nine-year-old virtuoso pianist, Franz Liszt, had the honour of playing before a glittering assembly of local nobility and connoisseurs of music in the home of Count Mihaly Esterhazy. His extraordinary skill, his ability to decipher the most difficult scores and to play at sight everything placed before him were beyond admiration and justify the highest hopes.

Such was the enthusiasm in Court circles that a committee was established, headed by Counts Apponyi, Szapary, and Erdody, to raise a subscription that was to guarantee the young prodigy the annual sum of six hundred Austrian florins for six years, to enable him to further his musical education in Vienna.

And so it was that Liszt, barely yet in his tenth year, left his native Hungary. The isolation of those early years in Raiding played an important part in the make-up of his character. The loneliness of his situation not only stimulated him to fill the long hours with practice at the piano, but gave him a life-long yearning for solitude that was to clash, sometimes violently, with the gay social life of the

travelling virtuoso of years to come. This early appreciation of solitude was encouraged by his deeply religious nature, fostered from an early age by his devout Catholic parents. The colourful pageantry of the religious ceremonies must have appealed as a relief from the dull monotony of village life. The wandering groups of Romany gypsies, with their vivid clothes, their infectious virtuoso music, and their riotous dances made zestful contrast to the flat monotonous landscape of this north-west corner of Hungary. Vivid impressions these, to charge the young imagination, and they were to have a lasting effect on Liszt throughout his life.

Vienna: musical capital of the day, city of Beethoven and Schubert, home of the two illustrious teachers of the keyboard, Hummel and Czerny. Adam Liszt went directly to see his friend, but found to his dismay that Hummel's fee was more than he could meet. Next he went to Czerny, Beethoven's greatest pupil, who agreed to teach the child for a fee of a florin a lesson, and even this he later refused to accept, such was his amazement at the boy's natural talent for the instrument, despite the rather doubtful means by which he achieved his ends:

He was a pale, weakly-looking child, and he swayed on the music stool as if he were drunk, so that I was often afraid he might fall. His playing was quite uncontrolled, undefined and confused, and he had so little notion of fingering that he flung his fingers all over the keys. I was therefore all the more astonished at the talent given him by nature. He played everything I put before him 'a vista' ['at sight'], entirely from instinct, showing all the more . . . that here Nature herself had produced a pianist! It was the same when, at his father's request, I gave him a theme for improvisation. Without the slightest knowledge of harmony, he still put a touch of genius into his interpretation.

Czerny proved to be an excellent choice as teacher. A strict disciplinarian, he tamed the 'natural' wilfulness of his young prodigy, forced him to consider every note, and laid the foundation of a piano technique that has remained a legend to this day. He concentrated his lessons on a series of endurance exercises—Clementi's *Gradus ad Parnassum*—and built up a manual dexterity and physique that could cope with any exigency. Years later Liszt was to pay eloquent tribute to this technical mastery in his formidable set of Transcendental Studies, which he dedicated to his Viennese teacher and friend, Carl Czerny.

Liszt was instructed in musical theory by that grand old Italian composer Salieri, who had influenced the careers of Mozart, Beethoven and Schubert before him. It was under him that Franz first began to compose, and at the age of eleven he contributed one of the fifty variations on a waltz theme commissioned by the publisher Diabelli.

Under Czerny's supervision Liszt gave several concerts in Vienna, sharing the stage with such artistes as Karoline Unger, and was forever stealing the notices: 'A young virtuoso has again dropped from the clouds and filled us with supreme admiration. It is almost unbelievable what this boy can do, considering his age . . . "Est deus in nobis" '

At the concert he played Hummel's Concerto in A Minor, a *Fantasia* composed by himself, and a transcription of Beethoven's Fifth symphony. Encouraged by the success of the latter the father sought to present his son to the 'Ageing Lion' himself. As Beethoven had a known dislike of child prodigies it was no easy matter to arrange, but finally, through the good offices of Beethoven's secretary Schindler, a visit to the composer's lodgings in Grinzing was accomplished. As at this stage in his life Beethoven was unable to hear even with the

aid of an ear trumpet, all communication was by way of the celebrated Conversation Books. An entry in Liszt's hand reads:

I have often expressed the wish to Herr von Schindler to make your high acquaintance, and am rejoiced, now, to be able to do so. As I shall give a concert on Sunday the 13th I most humbly beg you to honour me with your high presence.

Beethoven's replies were of course spoken, but judging by Schindler's entry a few pages later, it would seem that he rejected the invitation in a characteristically forthright manner:

Little Liszt has urgently requested me humbly to beg you for a theme on which he wishes to improvise at his concert tomorrow. He will not break the seal till the time comes.

The little fellow's improvisations must not be taken too seriously.

The lad is a fine pianist, but, so far as his fancy is concerned, it is far from the truth to say he really improvises.

Karl Czerny is his teacher.

Just eleven years.

Do come: it will certainly please Karl [Beethoven's young nephew] to hear how the little fellow plays.

It is unfortunate that the lad is in Czerny's hands.

You will make good the rather unfriendly reception of recent date by coming to little Liszt's concert. It will encourage the boy. Promise me to come.

Whether Schindler's advocacy was rewarded we do not know. Certainly Beethoven did not supply a theme for the improvisation, and being totally deaf at this time it would seem doubtful that he actually sat through the concert, though we have it on Liszt's own authority, later, that the great man climbed onto the platform and embraced the young musician, who was to become one of his most ardent champions.

It was Czerny who decided to call a halt to lessons. By the time Franz was twelve, the master felt that there was little more that he could teach his formidable pupil, who even then was being openly compared with Hummel and Moscheles, the two most universally acclaimed pianists of the age. Czerny advised that the boy should go to Paris to complete his musical education at the great Conservatoire there.

Left: Liszt's birthplace, the landsteward's tied house in Raiding
Below: The house as it stands today

No doubt with the example of Mozart in mind, father and son set forth on a tour of the cities of Germany *en route* for Paris. But first a farewell concert in Budapest: 'I am Hungarian and know no greater joy than to offer my homeland, before I set out for France and England, the first fruits of my training, as a first pledge of my heartfelt gratitude and thanks.' And so he repaid the subscription of his countrymen that had first enabled him to study in Vienna. And then to Paris by way of Munich—where he was kissed by the King— Augsburg, Stuttgart, Strasbourg; so many triumphant stages of his journey west where he dazzled and amazed in the manner of the infant prodigy some sixty years before him. 'A new Mozart has appeared . . . ' 'This fair-haired, handsome little boy displayed such skill, such lightness, feeling and strength, such signs of mastery, as to ravish and astound . . .'

But their reception at the Conservatoire in Paris soon soured the heady wine of success. Ironically it was the Italian director, Cherubini, who refused to relax the regulations which prevented foreigners from taking up a place at the Conservatoire. No letters of introduction from princes, no virtuosity at the keyboard could persuade him to change the rules. It was a bitter blow at the time, for Adam Liszt had set his hopes on the Conservatoire to polish the musical jewel that was his son.

It was the famous piano manufacturer Sébastien Érard, indignant at the Conservatoire's churlish intractability, who came to lend a timely hand, and advised Adam on the best teachers for his son—the Czech Antonin Reicha, a famous theorist who was to give him an ear for the authentic cadences of folk music and the fashionable Italian composer of light opera, Ferdinand Paër.

Perhaps even more important, Érard presented the boy with a model of his latest grand piano which incorporated his newest invention, the 'double-escapement', which made possible for the first time the rapid repetition of a single note. It was on an Érard that Liszt made his Paris debut in the Italian Opera on 8 March 1824. It was a sensation. The critic of *Le Drapeau* seems to have been quite carried away:

Since last night I believe in reincarnation. I am convinced that the soul and genius of Mozart is alive again in the body of young Liszt. It is Mozart himself.

His tiny arms can scarcely reach both ends of the keyboard, his feet can hardly touch the pedals, yet the child is beyond compare; he is the first pianist in Europe. Even Moscheles himself could not feel offended by this affirmation.

Paris took him to her heart. He was feted wherever he went. His portrait appeared in shop windows, his name was on every lip— 'Le Petit Litz', 'Putze', 'Zizy' as he was fondly known. Lionized by the ladies of the salons, he performed at no less than thirty six soirées in three months. The most splendid of these occasions was undoubtedly the evening given by the Duchesse de Berry, at which the entire royal family was assembled. But the position of a musician in the society of that epoch is accurately recorded by the Countess Marie d'Agoult in her '*Souvenirs*':

Composers and singers still had their place apart: in spite of the eagerness to have them, they appeared in the salons only on the footing of inferiors. If someone wanted to give a fine concert he went to Rossini, who for a recognized fee . . . undertook to arrange the programme and to see to the carrying out of it . . . The great maestro himself sat at the piano the whole evening, accompanying the singers. Generally he added an instrumental virtuoso—Herz or Moscheles, Lafont or Bériot, Naderman (the leading Paris harpist), Tulou (the King's first flute), or the wonder of the musical world, the little Liszt. At the appointed hour they arrived in a body and entered by a side door; in a body they sat near the piano; and in a body they departed, after having received the compliments of the master of the house and a few professed dilettanti.

It was Liszt who was to raise the status of the musician above that of the merely hired entertainer.

At this stage in his life there was an unhappy breakup of the Liszt household. His mother, Anna, a simple country woman at heart, found herself unable to adjust to the glittering world that had engulfed her family. Morbidly sensitive as to her lowly position in society, she separated from her husband when it became clear that she would not be able to accompany father and son on their forthcoming tour of England, and went off to live with her sister in Styria.

'Putzi's' London debut was given in the Argyll Rooms on 21 June 1824. With the general public it was an unqualified success, though he did meet with some jealous resentment from the rival clique of virtuosi as-

Above: The Casino at Sopron, where he played in public for the first time
Below: The Freyung in Vienna, 1822. Liszt stole the notices

Right: Liszt aged eleven—the legendary kiss from the deaf Beethoven

sembled: Clementi, Cramer, Ries, and Kalkbrenner. Only the great Moscheles did not feel offended by the astonishing mastery of a young rival and voiced his generous praise: 'In strength, and in his conquest of difficulties, he surpasses anything hitherto heard.'

Forthwith the Drury Lane Theatre was hired and the posters proclaimed that the child prodigy had 'consented to display his inimitable powers on the New Grand Piano Forte, invented by Sébastien Érard.' The business men were moving in. A year was knocked off his age; the boy was being taught the classic tricks of the showman.

So successful was this first visit to England that plans were laid for a second, the following year, after an extended tour of France. This time he travelled north to Manchester, where demand was such that he had to give a repeat performance, and thence across the sea to Ireland. But the crowning triumph came with a Royal Command Performance before King George IV at Windsor.

Shortly after his return to Paris, his one-act operetta *Don Sanche*—written under Paër's prompting to a libretto by Theaulon and de Rance—was given its premiere with a distinguished cast and lavish decors at the Academie Royale (L'Opera) on 17 October 1825, a few days before his fourteenth birthday. The excitement was immense but its success, as might be expected, was slight and short-lived, to be forgotten after its three performances. A more significant achievement in the field of composition at this time was the *Études en forme de douze exercises pour le piano*—Opus 1—written less for performance in public than as studies for his own self-education. These studies were far in advance of the most taxing of virtuoso concert pieces of this time and were to be the basis, later, of the famous *Études d'execution transcendante*.

Soirées in Paris; another tour of the French provinces; a third visit to England in 1827, the highlight of which was a performance for the Royal Philharmonic Society. Such incessant activity began to undermine his health. He returned to Paris exhausted, played out, a nervous wreck. Shocked by the mercenary exploits of the business men, disillusioned by the insincerity of so many of his fellow performers, grown weary of the empty virtuoso

ACADEMIE ROY
Les Bureaux s'ouvriront à 6 heures
Aujourd'hui L
(PAR EXT
La 1re

DON S

LE CHATE
Opéra e

LA DAN
Ballet-pantomime en 2 acte
Chant : M^{rs} Ad. Nourrit, Prévost ; Mmes
Danse dans l'Opéra : M. Paul ; Mme Mo
Danse dans le ballet : Mrs Milon, Ferdi
Mmes Anatole, Montessu, Elie, Hullin, Broc
LES ABONNEMENS ET TOU
S'adresser, pour la location des loges, au bureau de locatio

displays that he, the child prodigy, was called upon to make, he became moody, shunned applause, demanded solitude. The onset of puberty perhaps, but it was also a time of deepening artistic insight, and a resurgence of his powerful religious impulse. Much time was spent in prayer, and Franz indulged in penances and fastings which further sapped his strength. 'You belong to Art,' his father counselled, 'not to the Church'.

On doctor's advice Adam took his son to Boulogne to rest and recuperate by the sea. But it was Adam himself who was ill on arrival. Liszt wrote to his mother:

I am very troubled about Father. He was not well when we arrived, but his illness has got steadily worse, and today the doctor told me it could take a dangerous turn. He asks you to be brave, as he

himself believes he is very ill, and in this belief he has asked me to write to you in case you could come to France.

The Érards were at hand to comfort the stricken man and to console the son. Four days later, on 28 August 1827, Adam Liszt died of typhoid fever. The last words to pass his lips were a warning to his son: 'Je crains pour toi les femmes.'

Later in life Liszt was to recall the incident:

He said I had a good heart and did not lack intelligence, but he feared that women would trouble my life and bring me under their sway. This prevision was strange, for at that time, at the age of sixteen, I had no idea what a woman was, and in my simplicity I asked my confessor to explain the sixth and ninth Commandments to me, for I was afraid I might have broken them without knowing I had done so.

13

Chapter 2

Dead and Alive

When death took my father from me, and I returned to Paris alone, I began to think over what *art* could be, and what the *artist* must be, and I was overcome by the realisation of insuperable obstacles. . . . I developed a bitter aversion to art as I saw it practised: debased to not much more than a trade for the money it brings in, labelled as entertainment for fashionable society. I would sooner have done anything than be a musician in the service of some great lord, patronised and paid like a juggler or the clever dog Munito . . .

When Liszt's mother arrived in Paris towards the end of September 1827 she found that Franz had already sold his concert piano—ostensibly to raise the money to furnish his apartment in the Rue Montholon. Retired from the concert platform before the age of sixteen, he now earned his living as music teacher to the daughters of the aristocracy. His income from this alone was sufficient to keep himself and his mother in some style.

It was not to be long before his life was to be troubled by a woman, as his father had foreseen. His eye was caught by the fragile beauty of a pupil: Caroline Saint-Cricq, the dark-haired, blue-eyed sixteen-year-old daughter of the wealthy Comte Saint-Cricq, Minister of Commerce and Industry in the cabinet of Charles X. Lessons became more frequent, and visits to the house more prolonged as lessons merged into the reading of poetry, for it was Caroline who introduced him to the poems of Chenier and Lamartine, Victor Hugo and Dante. This idyllic romance was watched over, even encouraged, by Caroline's ailing mother for several months before she died, and her last plea to her husband is said to have been: 'If they love each other, let them be happy.' She must have known that the Comte had in mind a different marriage for their daughter, and shortly afterwards the young piano teacher was refused admittance to the house with the

curt explanation that the marriage had been arranged between Caroline and the Comte d'Artigaux. Liszt wrote and dedicated music to her, and many years later when making out his will, shortly before taking Holy Orders, he left her a special jewel that he had had mounted as a ring.

'I was ill for two years . . .', Liszt wrote later. Not only did the personal loss bite deep, but the ignominy of this barrier of class was a crushing blow to his self-esteem, and it was to colour his attitude to aristocracy from that time on. His immediate desire was to become a priest, and he hurled himself into a further period of religious crisis. His life became absorbed in the observance of strict religious duties, and he took to fasting. The effects on his health were even more acute than before and he began to suffer the cataleptic fits that had plagued his early childhood. After one attack he lay unconscious for three full days, and the rumour of his death prompted an obituary notice in *L'Etoile*:

The young Liszt has died in Paris. At an age when other children do not even think of going to school his talents had conquered the whole world . . . Liszt's guardian angel was his age, which protected him from every attack . . . 'He is only a child', people said, and envy remained dormant. If he had grown older and the spark within him had shone more brightly, the critics would have pounced on his faults, sought to diminish his merits, and would perhaps have brought bitterness into his life.

One of his few friends at this troubled time was the mystic Chrétien Urhan who encouraged Liszt to flirt awhile with the philosophies of Saint Simon. But of more lasting influence was his deep friendship with the Abbé Lammenais, who was a kind of spiritual father to him, and not only helped to clarify his religious thinking but also introduced him to the romantic literature of the day. With

Left: Franz Liszt in 1832, a lithograph by DeVeria
Below: The Abbé Lammenais

Byron and Chateaubriand, Constant and
Sénancour, Liszt shared the crises of the heart,
the will and the intellect, and enjoyed the
melancholic pangs of *le mal du siécle*.

The reverie was abruptly shattered. On
27 July 1830 he awoke to the sounds of
revolution, looked down from his window
at fighting in the streets. The terror and
bloodshed jolted him back to reality. 'The guns
have cured him', his mother succinctly put it.

But it was the artistic ferment of the following year that was truly to bring him back to
life again, to galvanize his wounded spirit.
In the course of this one year, 1831, Liszt
was to encounter all three of the musicians
whose example most influenced his artistic
development: Paganini, Berlioz and Chopin.

The legend of Nicoló Paganini had pre-
ceeded him to Paris: he had been famous in
Italy since the beginning of the century, but
had disappeared more than once for periods of
several years, only to emerge again even more
astonishing in technique and still more
mysterious in person; it was said that he had
been imprisoned for the murder of a former

wife, and during his solitary confinement over
a period of twenty years his 'soul' companion
had been a violin, broken and with but a single
string, from which he had wrested the innermost secrets. Even the most serious-minded
were prepared to believe that he had been
taught by the devil himself. And when he made
his Paris debut, on 9 March 1831, the excited
throng assembled at the Opera were in no way
to be disappointed.

Even at their first glimpse, as the strange,
gaunt figure glided menacingly forward to the
centre of the stage, the audience became
electrified. Here was an apparition to match
the wildest excesses of the Romantic imagination. Dressed from head to foot in black, here,
surely, was Mephistopheles himself: the
fleshless tortured body, even now ravaged by
the tubercular disease that finally killed him,
the aquiline nose, the haunted eyes, the
powerful forehead, the long lank mass of
raven-black hair, the brittle-thin fingers on
the violin . . .

And when he played it seemed as though the
devil was dancing on his bow. The unearthly

tones of his harmonics, the double trills, the thirds, the sixths, the octaves and tenths, the shimmering arpeggios, the cascades of glissandi, the bowed chords combined with a dancing pizzicato from the left hand . . . If a string should break, no matter, for he would continue on the remaining three—indeed a favourite trick was, after breaking the middle strings, to play a love duet on the two outer ones.

No one else played such music, for no one else could. And Paganini was careful to preserve his secrets. At rehearsals of a concerto his habit was to omit the cadenza so that any rival among the violins of the orchestra would hear it only once—at the public concert. He was never heard to practice any of his pieces, and spies who listened at his dressing-room door were rewarded, and puzzled, by short bursts of painful scratches and scrapings coming from within (the sounds of an exercise, in which he bowed upwards from underneath the strings, to develop both power and lightness in his bowing arm).

With such jealousy did Paganini guard his secrets that only rarely did he allow his compositions to be published. Many were to die with him, and it was only to demonstrate his powers that he was finally induced to publish his famous set of *Twenty four Caprices* —and it was only when they were eventually available for study in print that the full measure of his diabolic powers could be appreciated. It became Liszt's ambition to translate the virtuoso effects of the *Caprices* to the keyboard of the piano, while retaining the same technical problems that they posed on the violin—but how he did this will be discussed in a later chapter.

For Liszt the Paganini concert came as a blinding revelation. From Paganini he learned the art of showmanship, and perceived how a display of transcendental execution could establish the hold of a performer over his audience. As a virtuoso he stood alone. It was a challenge that Liszt could not fail to accept. He would become the Paganini of the piano:

For fifteen days my mind and my fingers have been slaving away like two damned souls. Homer, the Bible, Plato, Locke, Byron, Hugo, Lamartine, Chateaubriand, Beethoven, Bach, Hummel,

Mozart, Weber, are all around me. I study them, meditate on them, devour them feverishly. In addition, I work four or five hours at exercises (thirds, sixths, octaves, tremolos, repeated notes, cadenzas, etc). Ah, if only I don't go mad you will find in me an artist . . . What a man, what a violin, what an artist! God, what suffering, torture and pain in those four strings.

Liszt met Hector Berlioz on the eve of the first performance of the *Symphonie fantastique*, as Berlioz recalled in his *Memoires*:

I talked to him about Goethe's 'Faust', which he said he had not read, but about which he soon felt as enthusiastic as I. We felt a deep sympathy for each other, and the friendship between us grew ever closer and firmer. He attended the concert and attracted the attention of the entire audience by his applause and demonstrations of enthusiasm.

Throughout his life Liszt was to continue to champion this new-found friend. Later in Weimar he was to conduct performances of Berlioz' works, but now he set to work to make piano transcriptions of several of his compositions including the *Symphonie fantastique*. It was inevitable that Liszt should fall under the Berlioz spell, for this fiery genius had extended the expressive range of the orchestra in the way that Paganini had done that of the violin. And from Berlioz, too, he assimilated the dramatic possibilities of 'programme' music, while the *Faust* theme was later to provide the inspiration for one of Liszt's greatest masterpieces.

Liszt began once more to play in public, after an absence of several years. Like Paganini he returned with a still more amazing technique, a more mature artistic insight, and the panache of the emerging showman. Great were the enthusiasm and the applause. But in the midst of the hysteria and bravura display there was to come a new and calming influence.

Frederich Chopin had arrived from Poland. Only a year older than Liszt, he was already the completely formed musician—the poetic genius of the piano. As delicate and refined in his appearance as in his playing, Chopin soon won the hearts of the ladies of the salons and was welcomed into the aristocratic drawing rooms of Paris.

Both from Eastern Europe, Liszt and Chopin shared a common heritage, and the two pianists became close friends. Chopin introduced him to the nationalistic forms of the Mazurka and Polonaise. But more important, his refined and poetic playing of his own superbly pianistic compositions set an example which helped to check the worst excesses of Liszt's extravagance.

And it was through Chopin that Liszt was to meet the woman who was soon to play so decisive a role in his life. An impromptu party gathered at Chopin's apartment one evening in 1833. Berlioz and Liszt arrived together. Heine was there, and Delacroix, Rossini and Meyerbeer, George Sand, and the Countess Marie d'Agoult.

Chapter 3

Don Juan

Liszt was the centre of attention that evening. Chopin preferred to listen to his own music played by his friend, and Franz continued into the small hours. Marie, the Countess d'Agoult, has left a description of her first impression of him:

His flashing eyes, his gestures, his smile, now profound and of an infinite sweetness, now caustic, seemed intended to provoke me to an intimate assent ... With his slender figure, his pale complexion, his finely moulded face and his flowing hair, he seemed like a phantom for whom the hour when it must return to the darkness is about to sound.

Franz was evidently equally captivated by Marie, of whom George Sand said, 'Straight as a candle, white as a sanctified wafer', and he left his own description of her, penned many years later by his official biographer, Lina Ramann:

Beautiful, indeed very beautiful—a Loreley. Slender, of distinguished bearing, bewitchingly graceful and yet stately in her movements, with a proudly carried head covered with a profusion of blond hair that falls over her shoulders like a shower of gold, a profile of classic symmetry.

But when they spoke, the Countess noticed a certain something in his manner, a certain sensitivity to his position in society that must have smarted in him since the Saint-Cricq affair:

I had observed in the artist during our conversation an indefinable sense of umbrage, a kind of haste to remind himself of the difference in ranks, as if he were afraid that *he* would be reminded of it ... I felt embarrassed by this seeming superiority in my relations with a man whose immense talent and what I thought I already knew of his character placed him, in my esteem, so much above myself.

To assuage her sense of embarrassment the Countess straightway decided to invite the young pianist to her next reception, but found it anything but easy to draft the letter. She

was afraid that the common formulae of her world towards an artist not of that world would simply appear to be haughty, whereas to ignore these formulae might show more interest 'than was decorous in so novel a relation to a man so young and so much of a stranger to all my own people'. Characteristically Liszt, while accepting the invitation, did not send a written reply.

Marie Catherine Sophie de Flavigny, daughter of the Vicomte de Flavigny, was twenty eight when she first met Liszt. She had been married for six years to the Comte Charles d'Agoult, equerry to the Dauphin, a man more than twenty years older than herself. There had been three children of the marriage in as many years, and as quickly she had grown tired of him. Her husband cared not a fig for her intellectual interests and their indifference had soon grown to estrangement. By now she enjoyed complete independence, and having established herself as a leading figure in Paris literary and artistic circles, it was quite easy for her to invite the young pianist to her house. Franz was soon a frequent visitor. We can follow their story in Marie's own words for she wrote frankly of their relationship in her *Memoires*:

From the commencement our conversations were very serious and by common accord, quite free from anything banal ... We talked of the destiny of mankind, of its sadness and incertitude, of the soul and of God ... We said nothing that came too near the personal or the intimate, but the very tone of our talks showed that we were both exceedingly unhappy, and that, young as we were, we had been through more than one bitter experience.... Between us there was something at once very young and very serious, at once very profound and very naïve.

He would play for her, and in return she would read Goethe and Schiller to him. But soon there had to come a period of separation, for Marie was obliged, by family custom, to pass the summer with her children at her country estate at Croissy-en-Brie. Franz withdrew once more from society and plunged into his work with a passionate intensity. Six weeks later Marie invited him to stay in Croissy, and was clearly alarmed by a disagreeable change that had come over him. Their relations took on a new aspect:

If at bottom our talks remained the same as before, the tone of them had become something quite different. Franz brought to them a fantastic temper; I was ill at ease. Sometimes there would be long silences between us; at others Franz would talk with feverish animation, affecting a mock gaiety that made me uncomfortable . . . And strangely enough, his talent seemed to me as completely changed as his mind. When he improvised at the piano it was no longer as of old, to evoke suave harmonies that opened out the heavens to me; it was to set vibrating dischordant, strident tones from those powerful fingers of his.

Liszt's manner provoked an emotional scene from the Countess. She burst into floods of tears. Franz fell at her feet, imploring her forgiveness. All pretence between them was cast to the winds; they knew that each was destined for the other.

But the outward pretence had still to continue, even increase, and for the next twelve months they met infrequently—a fleeting moment at a Berlioz concert perhaps, a flying visit to Croissy, a careless hour of rapture at Liszt's apartment: 'Oh how ardent, how glowing on my lips is your last kiss!', Franz wrote, 'how heavenly, how godlike your sigh in my bosom. Marie, Marie, put your arms about my heart, your heart against my breast; clothe me wholly with your love.'

Their separation was accompanied by a suicidal anguish—*le mal de siécle*, the full Romantic agony:

I have not had a moment's tranquility since our separation. How many times has that terrible cry of the poet 'Horrible, horrible death!', lacerated my breast. Do not pity me. Let me weep a few days longer. Remain mine still; who else's hand could lay its benediction on my tomb?

Marie's reply was in similar vein:

I think of you wherever I am, whatever I may be doing. There have been days when I too have thought of suicide—but God had pity on me. Whatever my sufferings, present or to come, you

Above: The Countess d'Agoult, the first Muse
Below: Geneva, 1835, away from the storm

should not weep for them for they have brought me more good than you could know. You have succeeded in breaking all the bonds that still held me to the world, and have wakened in my soul a spirit of universal charity. May this thought be sweet to you in your dying hour.

And Franz continues:

Let us hope that God in His mercy and His infinite love will reunite us and absorb us wholly. I feel very weak and almost at death's door; we will revive, and our heads will burst the stone of the sepulchre ... Whatever may happen, we will love each other ...

These ardent protestations of love from Franz give the lie to that sorry chapter of falsehoods concerning the Countess d'Agoult in the Lina Ramann biography, written, as we shall see later, towards the end of Liszt's life and under the supervision of that other dominant woman in his life, the Princess Sayn-Wittgenstein, in which it was represented that Franz, the innocent young idealist, had been ensnared out of selfish vanity by an erotic, scheming older woman. The actual facts of the case were quite the opposite and Ernest Newman has established, beyond all doubt in my opinion, the essential truthfulness of Marie's own account.

In December of the year 1834, Marie's eldest daughter died of meningitis. Far from uniting the family, the tragedy only served to emphasize the disparity between husband and wife. Marie suffered terribly and came near to suicide. Liszt reacted in typical fashion, in the way he was always to do in time of moral crisis, and went into a religious retreat. For several months he sent no word of comfort to the Countess in her grief; and then suddenly a letter announced his intention of leaving France, and Europe, and hoping that he might see her once more before he left.

At their meeting, Franz, moved by her misery, proposed they should leave France together and persuaded her, as Marie has him say:

We have had enough of bending under the yoke that bows us down towards the earth; too long have we struggled and suffered in vain. Let us still struggle and suffer, but let it be together and erect. Our souls are not made for the things that can be shared, for those mute resignations in which everything is extinguished in tears. We are young, courageous, sincere, and proud. We need either great faults or great virtues; we must confess, in the face of heaven, the sanctity or the fatality of our love.

By March they must have been lovers in fact as well as by aspiration, for a child was born to them in December of that year. An elopement became a necessity, and by August 1835, the couple had set up house together in Geneva.

The scandal rocked Paris. The Comte d'Agoult remained indifferent. The lovers delighted to be together at last, alone in all the romantic grandeur and beauty of Switzerland. Marie was ambitious for him. She taught him *bon ton*, the ease and the grace and the refined manners of her aristocratic upbringing. It was she who concentrated his mind on composition and from this period comes the first of the *Années de pèlerinage: Suisse* and *Album d'un voyageur*. Each second day was set aside entirely for their readings together and Franz attended philosophy lectures at the University. But her dream of solitude *à deux* was not to last for long, for isolation did not suit him and he craved once more for the pleasures of society.

Soon their lodgings in the Rue Tabazan became the centre of a lively group of Bohemians: a few old acquaintances, but many new, drawn both by the playing of the celebrated virtuoso and the romantic exploits of the handsome young Don Juan. Liszt found it agreeable to be flattered once more, and was proud to display

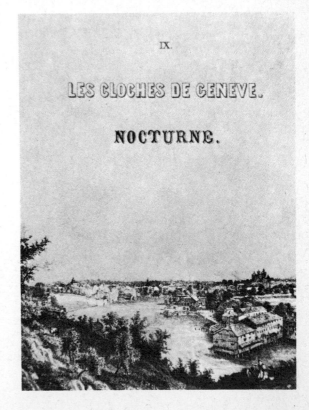

The title page of the nocturne 'Les Cloches de Geneve' from le Pèlerinage Suisse

his aristocratic conquest; though Marie, it seems, suffered acutely from the odium that attached to her union with a mere piano-player.

Liszt began to teach once more, giving his services free, at the newly opened Conservatoire in Geneva. The comments in his class-book concerning his pupils—all women—show a witty appreciation of their various attributes:

Mlle Demallayer, Marie: Vicious method (if there is any), great zeal, mediocre talent. Grimaces and contortions.

Mlle Calame, Amélie: Pretty fingers, work is diligent and careful, almost too much so. Capable of teaching.

Mlle Milliquet, Ida: an artist from Geneva. Languid and mediocre. Fingers good enough. Posture at the piano good enough. Enough 'enoughs', the grand total of which is not much.

Mlle Gambini, Jenny: Beautiful eyes.

On 18 December Marie was delivered of her nine-month burden, and the child was christened Blandine Rachel and registered as 'natural daughter of Franz Liszt, musician, and Cathérine Adelaide Méran, stockholder, both aged twenty four, unmarried, and domiciled in Geneva.' News of the birth travelled rapidly, and the added notoriety made any thought of Marie's return to her family impossible.

George Sand announced her intention of leaving Paris to join them. Recently divorced herself, the mistress of Chopin was all curiosity to see the scandalous couple in their exile. Her arrival coincided with a trip they had planned into the Alps with their friend the philosopher and orientalist Adolphe Pictet. George Sand followed them to Chamonix and tracked them down in the Hôtel de l'Union by means of Liszt's bizarre entry in the hotel register:

Place of birth . . .   Parnasus
Coming from . . .   Doubt
Journeying to . . .   Truth

In like style George Sand registered herself and her two children:

Right: Concert in Vienna, where Liszt once performed ten concerts in a month

Left: The new Ketten Bridge in Pest, built after the floods which took Liszt back to his homeland

Name of travellers ...	The Piffoëls family
Residence ...	Nature
Coming from ...	God
Journeying to ...	Heaven
Place of birth ...	Europe
Occupation ...	Idlers
Issued by ...	Public opinion

George Sand was quick to catch the care-free mood; and what a commotion they did make, this little band of Bohemians, with their long hair and eccentric clothes, their gay abandon, and their bombastic talk. George Sand herself helped spike the scandal, with her male attire, and her cigars and pipes. Their enthusiasms knew no bounds, their discussions were long and animated, their arguments heated and outspoken.

The days were spent tramping the valleys, or taking picnics beside the mountain streams. In the evenings, and often far into the night, Liszt improvised on the broken upright piano in his room, and as the champagne overflowed the others joined in, singing and stamping and clapping as he played: until the management burst in in alarm and complained that the other guests were packing up and leaving.

Liszt, now reaching the summit of his powers as a pianist and the first true blossoming of his art as a composer, seems to have imparted a certain electricity to the air, for so great was their enthusiasm that George Sand and Adolphe Pictet were both to write books about these ten days of high adventure on the slopes of Mont Blanc. Both left vivid accounts of their visit to the church of St Nicholas in Fribourg and the almost frightening impression that Liszt made upon them when he improvised on the organ a free and impassioned fantasy based on the plainsong of the *Dies Irae*.

But soon Liszt was to be called upon to display his prodigious powers before a vastly larger audience. News reached him of a serious threat to his career, a new challenge to his supremacy as a pianist. Sigismond Thalberg had taken Europe and Paris by storm and critics were already saying that his playing was superior to Liszt's and his compositions were finer than those of Chopin.

Liszt was not the man to leave it at that: 'I must go to Paris to assert myself against this upstart Thalberg. It is a question of *amour-propre*, nothing more, nothing less. I shall put a dash of water in the wine of Monsieur Sigismonde.'

The details of this 'contest of the gladiators' must wait till a later chapter, but the outcome of it was such an emphatic triumph for Liszt that Thalberg is scarcely ever to be heard of again.

After the battle was won, Liszt and the Countess decided to put into action their long discussed plans to visit Italy. Franz responded,

as Marie had hoped he would, to the great Italian art treasures, as well as the beautiful countryside and the balmy evenings, and began once more to compose. 'We often fled from the sweltering heat to the shade of the plane trees of the Villa Melzi', Liszt wrote, 'and read the Divine Comedy at the foot of Comolli's statue: Dante led by Beatrice. What a theme!'

In Bellaggio Liszt sketched the first draft of his great *Fantaisie, quasi Sonate: d'après une lecture de Dante*. And during this trip through Italy he completed the Twelve *Grandes Études Transcendantes* and the Six *Grandes Études d'après les Caprices de Paganini* and composed the second set of *Années de pèlerinage —Italie*. And here, at Bellaggio, their second child was born on Christmas day 1837, and named Cosima after the Lake Como.

When Marie recovered her strength the family moved south. In Milan, Liszt gave a concert at La Scala opera house and by the end of February they had settled down again, in Venice. But the idyll was not to last. In April the Danube over-flowed her banks, and Liszt read the harrowing reports of the terrible disaster that had beset the homeland he had almost by now forgotten. The letter he sent to the *Gazette Musicale* expressed his sense of shock:

Through this innermost tumult and feeling I learned the meaning of the word 'my father-land' . . . O my wild and distant country! O my unknown friends! O my great far-spreading family! Your cry of pain has brought me back to you. Touched to the depths, I bow my head, ashamed that I have forgotten you for so long . . . I left for Vienna on the 7th [April 1838]. I wished to give two concerts there: one for the benefit of my compatriots, the second to cover my travelling expenses, and then, alone and on foot, a knapsack on my back, to seek out Hungary in her remotest corners.

He had planned to give two concerts in Vienna in a month—he ended up by giving more than ten and playing at numerous soirées. For Liszt it was a personal triumph. In the heat of success he penned a tactless report to Marie in Italy:

It would be impossible to ask more in the way of satisfaction of one's vanity; the greatest people have not only received me with all possible consideration but have been the first to express the wish to meet me. As for the women—they are everywhere crazy about me.

And when he returned to Venice she found him much changed:

The way in which he spoke about his stay in Vienna brought me down from the clouds. The

27

women had thrown themselves at his head; he was no longer embarrassed by his lapses; he reasoned about them like a philosopher. He spoke of necessities . . . He was elegantly and expensively dressed; his talk was about nothing but princes; he was secretly pleased with his exploits as Don Juan . . .

One day she said something to hurt him. She called him a 'Don Juan parvenu', an upstart Don Juan. Stung by this Liszt countered by suggesting that Marie should take a lover, a certain Theodoro, whenever he was away. And when she would not hear of this, he tried to win her over to his plan to settle her in Paris with her family on the pretext that he would never expect her to endure the discomforts of the life of a travelling virtuoso. 'My family? Have I one now? Would my daughter recognise me?' Marie sobbed, the tears coursing down her cheeks, 'My only talent was my love for you, the desire to please you . . .'

The breach was healed for the moment. The family moved to Rome where a third child was born to them, a son who was christened Daniel. And it was in Rome that he formed a warm friendship with the painter Ingres, 'whose genius is inspired by an acute sense of beauty, impeccable taste and great enthusiasm'. It was Ingres who widened Liszt's perception of the great Italian masters:

Art in all its grandeur displayed itself to my astonished gaze. Each day I grew more convinced that a hidden relationship linked the works of geniuses. Raphael and Michelangelo helped me to understand Mozart and Beethoven; in the works of Giovanni di Pisa, Fra Beato and Francia I found explanations for Allegri, Marcello and Palestrina; Titian and Rossini appeared to me as twin stars . . . Dante found an artistic echo in the work of Orcagna and Michelangelo; one day he may find musical expression in some Beethoven of the future.

And under Marie's supervising eye he settled down to compose once more, working on the 'Petrarch' Sonnets and completing the 'Dante' Sonata. But he was restless at heart and the family took once more to the road: from Rome to Pisa and on, via Lucca, to the tiny fishing village of San Rossore. It was here that Liszt received the news that a public subscription for a Beethoven monument in Bonn had amounted to only the trifling sum of 424 francs 90 centimes (about £30). Angered by such a display of public apathy towards his idol,

and with a gesture characteristic of his generosity, he pledged himself to raise the cost of the marble (estimated at 60,000 francs) by giving a series of six concerts in Vienna. He stipulated only that the commission for the work should be given to the sculptor Bartolini, who had recently completed a fine marble bust of Liszt himself in Rome.

Marie's farewell words reveal the agitation of her heart:

Take care of my love, if you can; it is yours as completely now as ever in the old days. I fear that trouble will come from the fact that you can no longer endure to hear the truth and that you are unwilling to submit to any curb. The only language you have been willing to listen to is the language of flattery. I cannot believe that a man ought to surrender himself blindly to all his instincts.

Liszt was greeted in Vienna with wild enthusiasm. In a short time he had assured the costs of the Beethoven monument, and started to amass his personal fortune. He was welcome in the homes of the most illustrious families in the land, and entertained extravagantly in return. 'I am throwing a veritable aristocratic supper,' he reported back to Marie, spacing out the names for her benefit:

Prince PÜCKLER
Prince Fritz SCHWARZENBERG
Count APPONYI
Count HARTIG
Baron REISCHACH
Count SZÉCHENI
Count WALDSTEIN
Count Paul ESTERHAZY

'It will be a little frigid, perhaps—but in the best style!'

But the triumph in Vienna was as if only a prelude to his Hungarian home-coming. In Pest the tumultuous reception reflected a nation's heartfelt thanks for the flood-relief concerts he had given the year before: and the concerts he now gave in Pest were almost exclusively devoted to various charities—the National School of Music and the National Theatre among them. After the final concert he was presented with a sword of honour. He accepted it with the words:

This sword, once used so heroically in defence of our country, has in this hour been given into frail and peaceable hands. Is it not a symbol? Is it not to say, gentlemen, that Hungary, having covered itself with glory on so many battlefields, now calls on the arts, on literature, on the sciences, all partisans of peace, to provide new examples? Is it not to say that those who toil with their minds and their hands also have a noble task, a high mission to fulfil amongst you?

He was to remember these words a few years later when Hungary was torn apart by bloody revolution.

But for the present he was acclaimed whenever he ventured into public. When he entered his box at the National Theatre in Pest for a performance of Beethoven's *Fidelio*, 'the whole audience rose and clapped and shouted "Éljen, Éljen!" I acknowledged the applause three times, no more, no less, in the style of a king.'

But Marie, left at home with the three small children, was not so impressed. In her *Memoires* she lamented; 'Franz abandoned me for such small motives! It was not to do a great work, not out of devotion, not out of patriotism, but for salon success, for newspaper glory, for invitations from princesses.'

The climax of his early tours came in Berlin, where he gave twenty concerts in a little under three months. The women fell over themselves for his favours and he was in constant demand at the fashionable soirées. His triumphant departure from Berlin in March 1842 had the poet Rellstab writing:

He marched out not *like* a king but *as* a king, ringed round with a rejoicing crowd, a king in the imperishable kingdom of the Spirit.

He returned to Marie from time to time during his travels. For a summer retreat he rented a house on the island of Nonnenwerth, situated in the middle of the Rhine a little above Bonn. Here they were able to recapture some of their earlier happiness in these peaceful surroundings. But the summer months seemed quickly over and Liszt resumed his travels once more.

He roamed Europe for seven years, giving concerts modelled on the example of Paganini the decade before. We read of Liszt in London and Edinburgh and Cork: in Copenhagen and Constantinople: in Poland and Portugal, Spain and Russia: France, Germany, and, of course, Hungary. Europe was criss-crossed by his travels. He triumphed everywhere, and his vanity knew no bounds.

He was decorated by nearly every court in Europe and the cartoonists had a field day depicting him at the piano weighed down with his sword and medals. His personality and artistry had helped to break down all barriers of class—the piano-player was now accepted as an equal in all the best circles. In his arrogance he could be aggressive—reflecting even still, perhaps, that 'indefinable sense of umbrage' that Marie had noticed when she had first met him—and he would sometimes assert his position by being deliberately rude even to those of the highest rank if he felt they were not paying the attention to him that he considered his due. The story has been often told of how he abruptly stopped playing when Czar Nicholas I of Russia continued to talk during a performance. When the Czar enquired why the music had ceased, Liszt replied sarcastically: 'Music herself should be silent when Nicholas speaks!'

Right: The princess Belgiojoso who arranged the celebrated clash of the giants, Liszt and Thalberg, on the 31st March 1837 (see page 54)
Far right: Camille Pleyel

Marie complained, 'but I will not be one of your mistresses. Try at least to spare me the public vulgarities. This persistent moral drunkeness will lead to a decay of the soul, a disgust for all natural affection.'

But there were to be many others: the Princess Belgiojoso, the singer Caroline Unger, the pianiste Camille Pleyel . . . and 'La Dame aux Camélias', Mariette Duplessis. On hearing of her death, in April 1847, Liszt, who was never it seems to learn tact in these matters, wrote to Marie:

I never told you what a singular attachment I entertained for this lovely creature when I was last in Paris. I told her I would take her with me to Constantinople . . . And now she is dead. And I know not what strange chord of antic elegy vibrates in my heart when I remember her.

And when Marie complained once more he tried to heal the wound:

When I first left you, to go to Vienna—that was my crime, and is my profound sorrow . . . I have conceived a disgust for my piano; I wish I could play for you alone; I do not know why the crowd listens to me and pays me. The acclamations of the crowd, the intoxications and excesses of my life, and the banal and lying embraces of my mistresses in Vienna, in Hungary, in Trieste, everywhere indeed, have resounded the pitiless funeral bell of that fatal hour when I left you.

But Marie knew better, by now, than to be fooled by it all, and in 1847 she wrote to him bringing their relationship finally to an end:

What have I to do with a charming good-for-nothing, an upstart Don Juan, half mountebank, half juggler, who makes ideas and sentiments disappear up his sleeve, and looks complacently at the bewildered public that applauds him? Ten years of illusion! Is that not the very sublime of extravagance? Adieu; my heart is bursting with bitterness.

And the women everywhere clamoured for his attentions. In the number of his conquests he must rank as a serious rival to the Don himself. Stories of his liasons reached Marie from one town after another; stories of his affairs with this woman or with that which were often relayed to her by Franz himself: 'I see quite a lot of two women here,' he wrote from Berlin, 'Bettina von Arnim and Charlotte Hagn. The first has turned herself into the sublime servant of genius [an emotional and capricious woman, she had disturbed the peace of mind of both Beethoven and Goethe before him]: she is an imp of magnetic intelligence. The second has been the odalisque of two kings; in talent she is the German Mlle. Mars, I think.'

The great scandal was caused by his affair with that tempestuous dancer Lola Montez, whose antics brought about the abdication of King Ludwig I of Bavaria. Liszt quickly tired of her, and made good his escape to another town by bribing the porter to lock her in their hotel room. But Lola was not to be got rid of so easily. She wreaked her revenge at a dinner given in Liszt's honour in Bonn, following the unveiling of the Beethoven memorial, by bursting into the hall and executing one of her celebrated erotic dances on the table.

'I have no objection to being your mistress,'

And in her bitterness the Countess, under her nom-de-plume Daniel Stern, made public her affair with Liszt in the biographical novel *Nelida* (the title itself is an anagram of Daniel). She spared him nothing in the directness of her style, and her critical observations of his weak and divided character. The novel did him no little harm in Germany, and he was deeply hurt by Marie's portrait of him, no less because of the essential truth of it. Though on the face of it he claimed that he was pleased at its 'business success', it was later to be the cause of a bitter rift between them. When the second edition was brought out in 1866 Liszt wrote: '. . . the character of Guermann is a stupid invention'. And as a 'stupid invention', an unjust attack by a scorned woman, it was to be considered by all early Liszt biographers until Ernest Newman's penetrating study in 1934.

Shortly after the publication of the novel in 1847, Liszt started out on his third tour of Russia. Among the audience at a charity concert in Kiev was the young Princess Carolyne von Sayn-Wittgenstein. She made a large donation to the charity and Liszt duly called on her the next day to thank her for her generosity. A bond was forged between them at that meeting and the Princess swamped him during the remainder of his tour with a series of bombastic letters that literally shrieked her love in his face:

I kiss your hands and kneel before you, prostrating my forehead to your feet, laying, like the Orientals, my finger on my brow, my lips, and my heart, to assure you that my whole mind, all the breath of my spirit, all my heart exist only to bless you, to glorify you, to love you unto death and beyond—beyond even death, for love is stronger than death.

Nothing daunted by such histrionics, Liszt returned to Kiev at the end of his tour and stayed with the Princess at Woronice, the largest of her estates. She was twenty-eight, and plain, and married; but Liszt was flattered by the aristocratic title, dazzled by her fortune, overwhelmed by her culture and intellect, overpowered by the forcefulness of her character and strength of will, and, perhaps most important of all, found benediction in her intensely religious nature.

This visit to Woronice marked an important turning point in Liszt's career. He renounced the life of a travelling virtuoso and never again did he earn a single penny for himself by his piano playing. Having earned in a few years a sufficient fortune to keep himself in comfort for the rest of his life, he felt drawn to fulfil his destiny as a composer.

In 1848 he settled in Weimar, where for several years past he had held the position of Honorary Kappelmeister at the Grand-Ducal Court. His duties bound him for only three months a year, leaving the other nine free for composing or for travel. He had an orchestra at his disposal and complete freedom in the choice of opera productions and concert programmes.

As for the Princess, he seems temporarily to have forgotten her, and evidently it came as a rude shock to him to find that Carolyne had pursued him there, if we are to believe the account of Carolyne's later friend at Court, Frau von Plötz:

Liszt has treated the Princess badly . . . the originality, the intellect, the millions and the title of the Princess attracted him; but all that was in his mind was a liason of the usual kind, with the usual vows of love, but with each party knowing from the commencement precisely what it all meant. She however took the matter very seriously . . . He had probably forgotten the matter, and was living here in Weimar in a hotel with another woman—the ordinary Parisian *femme entretenue*; . . . Suddenly, to his horror, he receives a letter from Carolyne, telling him that she has made the sacrifice, and that all that remained was for him to meet her at the frontier. He *had* to fetch her, for he could not get out of it—conventional honour forbade that; but he *did* want to get out of it. He did everything in his power to try to persuade her to terminate the relation, for without her millions . . . Carolyne did not suit him. She never complains, but I have often seen her in tears.

The Princess settled in the Altenburg Palace; Liszt remained at the hotel; the *femme entretenue* was sent packing back to Paris. After a tactful interval Liszt joined the Princess in the Altenburg, to the distress of the local townsfolk. The Princess was never to be very popular in Weimar, treated even as an object of suspicion on account of her strange clothes and incessant cigar-smoking, and was derisively referred to as 'The Mistress of the Honorary Kapellmeister'.

In his *Memoires*, Theodor von Bernhardi, the famous politician and historian, has left a character sketch of the Princess and Liszt together:

She is a small, dark, ugly, sickly, very clever and adroit Polish woman with a slightly Jewish nuance. She is very indiscreet and asks a great many personal questions, hoping by this means to acquire a certain ascendancy, so that people will not venture to injure her in any way . . . It is wonderful how completely Carolyne has brought Liszt to her feet . . . She has ensnared him by his vanity; she strews incense about him perpetually, without proportion and without scruple . . . He is not a man of transcendent intelligence, though he has a certain 'worldly wisdom' and his good nature makes him likeable enough. He is a weak character, who lets things go as they will; but Carolyne is ambitious for him; she wants to make something of him, and no doubt dreams of playing a role herself in it all.

And that is precisely what she did. For twelve years in Weimar she did her own work in the same room as him, encouraging Liszt to settle down and stay at his desk. Under her tutelage he composed the great majority of his most important works—the Piano Sonata in B minor, the two Piano Concertos, the *Hungarian Rhapsodies*, the Symphonic Poems, the 'Dante' Symphony, and the finest of all his works, the 'Faust' Symphony. And under Liszt Weimar became the fountain-head of the revival of German culture.

In his relations with the Princess the impression was always conveyed that their love was strictly platonic, though Carl Maria Cornelius, son of the composer and Liszt's secretary in Weimar, knew otherwise: 'There were three children of the union, who were born in other towns than Weimar and brought up in Brussels.'

Ever since she arrived in Weimar the Princess had been negotiating for a divorce, on the grounds that she had been a minor at the time of her marriage and an unwilling party to the contract. However her husband, and more especially his relatives, were not inclined to let so large a fortune slip through their fingers and pulled every string, political and religious, to retain it. But the Princess was busy pulling her own strings, and her influence with her cousin the Czar looked like bringing about the divorce. In 1860 she went to Rome to apply fresh pressures on the Vatican authorities to hurry through the annulment.

Liszt stayed behind for a while sorting out his papers and putting his affairs in order. The final year in Weimar had not been an entirely happy one. His artistic plans for Weimar had been frustrated—he had even been hissed after a performance of Cornelius's opera *The Thief of Bagdad*, which he had taken as a personal insult. Added to his artistic disappointments, there had been the personal grief of the death of his son Daniel. Alone now in Weimar he was moved to write his will:

This is my testament—

I write it on the date of 14th September [1860] when the Church celebrates the elevation of the Holy Cross. The name of this feast also expresses the ardent and mysterious emotion which, like sacred stigmata, has transpierced my entire life.

Yes, Christ crucified, the 'foolishness' and the elevation of the Cross, this was my true vocation. I have felt it to the depths of my heart from the age of seventeen, when with tears and supplications I begged to be permitted to enter the

seminary in Paris, and I hoped that it would be given to me to live the life of the saints and perhaps die the death of the martyrs. It has not been so, alas! But never since, through the many sins and errors that I have committed and for which I am sincerely repentant and contrite, has the divine light of the Cross been wholly withdrawn from me. Sometimes it has even flooded my whole soul with its glory. I thank God for it, and I shall die with my soul attached to the Cross, our redemption, our supreme beatitude; and to render a testimony to my faith, I desire to receive the sacraments of the Catholic, Apostolic and Roman Church before my death, and thus obtain the remission and absolution of my sins.   Amen.

Whatever good I have done and thought for twelve years, I owe to Her whom I have so ardently desired to call by the sweet name of wife—which human malignity and the most deplorable machinations have obstinately opposed hitherto—to Jeanne Elizabeth Carolyne, Princess Wittgenstein, born Iwanowska.

I cannot write her name without an ineffable thrill. All my joys have come from her, and my sufferings will always go to her to find their appeasement. She has not only associated and identified herself completely and without respite with my existence, my work, my cares, my career— aiding me with her advice, sustaining me with her encouragement, reviving me by her enthusiasm with an unimaginable prodigality of pains, previsions, wise and gentle words, ingenious and persistent efforts; more than this, she has still more often renounced herself, sacrificed what was legitimately imperative in her own nature in order the better to carry my burden, which she has made her wealth and her sole luxury.

I should have liked to possess an immense genius in order to celebrate this sublime soul in sublime harmonies. Alas, only with difficulty can I succeed in stammering a few scattered notes which the wind carries away. If, nevertheless, something remains of my musical labours (at which I have toiled with a dominant passion for ten years),

Liszt's library and music-room at the Altenburg, Weimar

may it be the pages in which Carolyne, through the inspiration of her heart, has played the greatest part.

I beg her to pardon me for the sad insufficiency of my works as an artist, as well as for the still more distressing insufficiency of the good intentions that have been mingled with so many failures and incongruities. She knows that the most poignant sorrow of my life is not to have felt myself sufficiently worthy of her, not to have been able to raise myself, to maintain myself firmly in that pure and holy region which is the abode of her spirit and her virtue.

At the same time that I owe to Carolyne the little good that is in me, I owe her also the small share of material goods that I possess—in a word, the little that I am and the very little that I have. She has assumed the burden of the conservation, the augmentation, and the regular investing of the funds that constitute my heritage, amounting to about 220,000 francs [£15,000]. I beg Carolyne to see that this heritage which I leave is divided as simply as possible in equal parts between my two daughters, Blandine and Cosima. It will be, of course, understood that the small annuity which my very dear mother, Mme Anna Liszt, in Paris, has drawn for a number of years from the interest of my property, is to be preserved for her intact.

. . . Finally, I ask Carolyne further to send from me to Mme Caroline d'Artigaux, born Countess de Saint-Cricq (at Pau), one of my talismans mounted in a ring.

And now I once more fall on my knees with Carolyne to pray, as we have often done together.

I desire to be buried simply, without any pomp, and, if possible, at night.

After Weimar Liszt went off to Paris and tasted once more the freedom and pleasures of a bachelor life. His letters to the Princess are full of the most abject desolation at her absence, and 'if he wept on the side of his face that he turned towards Carolyne,' as Cornelius so charmingly phrased it, 'he certainly did his best to smile with the other.'

Meanwhile, in Rome, Carolyne had managed to accomplish her task at the Vatican and preparations for the marriage were finally taking shape. A decree of annulment was drawn up and the ceremony fixed for 22 October 1861, Liszt's fiftieth birthday. Liszt dutifully travelled to Rome, though the perspicacious Cornelius saw that it was all 'simply a blague':

His nature was the last in the world to be suitable for marriage; and to tie himself to an ageing woman was more than could be expected of him. He still wanted to be chivalrous, or at any rate

appear to be so, and outwardly made it look as if he were willing to fall in with Carolyne's plan for marriage. But in Rome he was so undisguisedly cold towards her that the woman in her compelled her to renounce her plan.

Cosima, too, said that her father looked forward to the marriage 'as to a burial service', and this state of mind was confirmed by Carolyne herself:

When Franz arrived in Rome in October I was conscious of the change in him. He had become indifferent; the thought of a legal union with me no longer appealed to him as a necessity.

In the end he was saved by the bell. The tiny church of San Carlo al Corso was already bedecked with flowers for the occasion, but on the very eve of the wedding day relatives of Prince Sayn-Wittgenstein demanded a postponement on the grounds that new evidence had come to light which must first be carefully studied: but what this new development was has never been divulged.

Only much later, and to her utter astonishment, did Carolyne learn that her husband, Nicholas, had obtained a divorce from her in Russia as far back as 1855 and had kept it secret from her. When he died in 1864, and there was no possible obstacle to her union with Liszt, it was already too late:

Liszt had never asked me again whether the marriage was possible or not. He was of course ready at any time to stand before the altar with me, but I knew that if he did so it would be to fulfil a duty. And so I never spoke of it to him again.

The Princess was broken by this failure of her marriage plans after a struggle lasting nearly fifteen years. To the end of her days she was to lead the life of a recluse, shut up in her small apartment in the Via del Babuino, with the windows closed and the curtains permanently drawn. She had become a religious crank. In her contempt for the Church, she worked incessantly, while she smoked her cigars, at her mammoth literary attack on the Vatican authorities which she titled *The Interior Causes of the External Weaknesses of the Roman Catholic Church*. Virtually unreadable, it ran to twenty-four volumes, each of over a thousand pages. It occupied entirely the last twenty-five years of her life. She completed the final volume at the end of February, 1887, and a fortnight later she died.

Chapter 4

Mephistopheles Disguised as a Priest

'The Princess is living a sad and restricted life in Rome', Cornelius recorded in his diary for 1862, 'and I pity this poor woman from the bottom of my heart. Liszt, I am afraid, has had the impulse to soar destroyed in him, for with the Princess he has lost the very nerve of his life. His power to achieve the best in him will fail, and he will go under. It makes me sad at heart.'

Cornelius was a better prophet than he knew. Without the Princess's strong personality to guide him, Liszt's life soon lost its true direction. The great art historian Gregorovius made his acquaintance at about this time and wrote in his *Roman Journal* under the date of 13 April: 'Liszt: a striking demonic figure—tall, gaunt, with long grey hair. Madame S. was of the opinion that he was burnt out, that only the walls were still standing, in which there flickered a ghostly flame.'

In times of moral crisis, his thoughts were wont to turn to religion. In his Will he had confessed that he felt the Church to be his true vocation: now, he wrote to his mother:

You know, dearest mother, how during the years of my youth, I dreamed myself incessantly into the world of the saints. Nothing seemed to me so self-evident as heaven, nothing so true and so rich in blessedness as the goodness and compassion of God. When I now read the lives of the saints I feel I am meeting again, after a long journey, old and revered friends from whom I shall never part.

And then in September news came from Paris of another personal tragedy, the death in childbirth of his elder daughter, Blandine. It deepened the mental anguish and plunged Liszt into the very depths of despair. They were the blackest months of his whole life. It hastened the physical changes of old age, and in a few months his hair turned white, and the warts

that are such a prominent feature of the later photographs came out on his face.

Liszt found some measure of solace in the beautiful little monastery of the Madonna del Rosario on the Monte Mario, living as guest of the Dominican friars. Situated on one of the hills, it commanded beautiful views across Rome, and Michelangelo's dome on St. Peter's could be seen breaking the outline of the hill to the west. Even encroached upon by modern buildings as it is today, it still maintains its mood of serenity and repose.

He had a harmonium in his cell with him, and it was here that Pope Pius IX came to ask him to play for him. Janka Wohl wrote down Liszt's own account of the Pope's visit:

The Holy Father was sad, and directly he arrived he gave Liszt to understand that he had come on purpose to be cheered up by his talent. He begged him to improvise. He also was particularly fond of this kind of music, maintaining that the originality

Right: 'The Law, my dear Palestrina, ought to employ your music . . . in order to lead hardened criminals to repentance'. Pope Pius IX visits the Abbé in his cell. (Note the artist's grand harmonium!)

37

and the individuality of the artist was more clearly marked when nothing fettered the inspiration of his soul. 'I played, therefore,' said the master, 'as the spirit moved me. Perhaps my sympathetic hearer inspired me; but, without wishing to praise my "strumming", I must tell you that the Holy Father was deeply affected and when I had finished he said rather a curious thing to me:

"The law, my dear Palestrina, ought to employ your music, if, however, she could get it otherwise than in this spot, in order to lead hardened criminals to repentance. No one could resist it, I am sure; and the day is not far distant, in these times of humanitarian ideas, when similar psychological methods will be used to soften the hearts of the vicious."

He broke his retreat to attend a music festival at Carlsruhe, at the request of his famous pupil Hans von Bulow, the husband of his only surviving child, Cosima. From there he paid brief visits to Weimar and Paris before returning to Rome to complete his preparations for the priesthood at the monastery of the Lazzaristi.

But first he 'gave his farewell concert in the Palazzo Barberini', Gregorovius wrote; 'He played the *Invitation to the Waltz* and the *Erl King*, a curious farewell to the world. No one suspected that he had the Abbé's stockings already in his pocket.'

The next day Liszt went into retreat. A letter to the Princess catalogued the events of days passed in meditations: he rose at half-past six, meditated alone in his cell for an hour; coffee was brought to him in his room, after which he attended Mass at half-past eight. The morning was divided between solitary readings of the scriptures and visits to the Holy Sacrament. He ate a spartan lunch in the refectory at midday, sitting alone at a little table, listening to the readings of the monk from the pulpit. Walks in the garden and more readings from the Bible filled the afternoon. A solitary supper in silence was followed by religious discussions with the Father Superior until lights out at ten.

'The following Sunday [25 April 1865]', Gregorovius continues, 'Liszt received the tonsure in St. Peter's and first consecration at the hands of Mgr. Hohenlohe. He now wears the Abbé's frock, and, as Schlözer told me yesterday, looks well and contented. This is the end of the gifted virtuoso, a truly sovereign personality. I am glad that I heard him play again; he and the instrument seem to be one, as it were a *piano-centaur*.'

Liszt in fact received only four of the seven degrees of priesthood: he was doorkeeper, reader, acolyte and exorcist. In addition he was an honorary canon, but he could neither celebrate Mass, nor hear Confession. He could leave the priesthood whenever he desired and kept his options open even to marry if he so wished.

Immediately after the ceremony Liszt moved into his new apartment, within the Vatican itself, opposite the famous Logia of Raphael. That night he dined and smoked cigars and drank his cognac with the Princes of the Church. He was still the Liszt of old.

'I think I need hardly tell you that I have not changed to any extent', he wrote to one of his mistresses, Agnes Street-Klindworth, 'still less have I forgotten anything. It is only that my life is ordered more simply—and that the Catholic devotion of my childhood has become a regular and guiding sentiment.'

Yet for Liszt this step into the priesthood was no pretence—it was done with the utmost sincerity and with characteristic intensity. A little later he wrote:

Convinced as I was that this act would strengthen me in the right road, I accomplished it without effort, in all simplicity and uprightness of intention. Moreover, it agrees with the antecedents of my youth . . .

To speak familiarly, if 'the cloak does not make the monk', it also does not prevent him from being one; and, in certain cases, when the monk is already formed within, why not appropriate the outer garments of one?

But I am forgetting that I do not in the least intend to become a monk, in the severest sense of the word. For this I have no vocation.

But his friends, remembering the medals and sword, the illegitimate children, not to mention the scandal of Lola Montez, were inclined to treat it as the final *coup de th éatre* of the showman.

Schlözer declared that 'It was only one of his bizarreries for the benefit of the world, to make people talk about him,' and Gregorovius voiced the thoughts of many when he said: 'Yesterday I saw Liszt clad as an Abbé. He was getting out of a hackney carriage, his black silk cassock fluttering ironically behind him. Mephistopheles disguised as a priest. Such is the end of Lovelace.'

Liszt remained less than a month in his Vatican apartment. A richly furnished suite of rooms, with a grand piano, in the Villa d'Este in Tivoli was put at his disposal by his close friend, the newly elected Cardinal, Mgr. Hohenlohe. The garden of the Villa d'Este is one of the most beautiful in the world, with its giant Cypresses and terraced water gardens. Here, amid the music of a hundred fountains and the early morning chorus of the birds, Liszt found the peace and solitude he needed to compose.

But, unable to bear for long his priestly isolation, Liszt made the first of what were to become annual pilgrimages to his own shrine at Weimar, where he could vaunt himself in aristocratic society and indulge his love of flattery. His female admirers were clearly delighted there was so little change in him, and one of them, Adelheid von Schorn, even penned an apologia on his behalf:

Liszt knew best what he was doing when he remained a man of the world even after becoming an Abbé; a point that distressed the Princess, who would have prefered him to work for the glory of God. Liszt *could not* be always composing; he needed outer stimulants, he needed the world. When he was in the mood to write serious things he was happy to be doing so; but the mood was not always there. Every true artist knows that it must be so.

And even as a priest he was prey to the affairs of the heart and the weakness of the flesh. The most celebrated of these affairs was his passionate liason with Olga Janina, the fiery 'Cossack Countess'. A wild horsewoman from the steppes of the Ukraine, Olga was possessed by a violent temperament. She had married at fifteen, horse-whipped her husband and left him the very next day. At sixteen she was mother of their child. A beautiful Cossack girl with 'a pale intelligent face and large black eyes', she was only nineteen when she sought Liszt out in Rome in 1869, having become infatuated by his music which she had studied at the Conservatoire in Kiev.

They seem to have been immediately fascinated by each other. He was flattered by her adulation of his music, and she was captivated by his charm. Then suddenly Liszt launched into an impassioned performance of Chopin's Polonaise in C sharp minor, that can only have

been calculated to win an impressionable young heart. Olga remembered afterwards his 'smile that was like a shaft of sunlight'.

She attended his Friday master-class and was shocked by the behaviour of the other pupils, with their fathers, mothers, cousins and aunts all of whom covered his hands with 'long and unctuous kisses'. She alone desisted, and was greeted coldly in return. Later that evening to her great astonishment Liszt appeared at her apartment and apologised for his rudeness. 'He was no longer the same man. He took my head between his hands and kissed it.' In the future he received her in his apartment on Tuesdays as a private pupil. Olga worked hard to please him, and helped him by copying out his music, winning his admiration on account of the beauty of her caligraphy.

One day she told him that she loved him. Liszt enfolded her in his arms, then said in a low voice 'Never speak to me of love: I must not love'. Although she despised him for his vanity and love of worldly luxury, she determined to play on it in order to bring him to her feet. She moved into a large and expensive apartment in Rome, and travelled to Paris especially to have an entire wardrobe created for her by Worth, the most fashionable couturier in the world at that time. In two years she was to spend not only her own considerable fortune, but also the legacy that should really have belonged to her child. She wore one of her Worth creations to a reception in Rome and the trick worked: 'When I saw how enchanted, almost tender, he was, putting his arm round my waist before them all, by way of establishing his intimacy with the rich Countess who had come to Rome from the depths of the Ukraine in order to find him— he who, had I arrived in my Cossack clothes, would barely have noticed me—I could not repress a feeling of rage.'

And soon there was another intimate scene between them. ' "I ought not to love; but I do love and cannot conceal it. I beg you"— and here his voice became so caressing that I trembled from head to foot—"to have pity on me now that you have torn this confession from me. Let your love be sweet to me; do not let it make me perjure myself . . . Call me Ferencz", he said; "*tutoi* me"; and he covered me with passionate kisses.'

The next day, troubled by the dangers of an intimate relationship, Liszt fled to his retreat in Tivoli. Playing on a weakness she had observed in his character, she let him be for several weeks; then, dressed as a garden-boy, carrying a basket of flowers, she gained admittance to his suite. 'He showed such joy that I could see how terribly solitude weighed on his soul that was so passionately in love with the world and its homage.' A few days later her aim was achieved. He turned the key in his lock, enclosed her in his arms, and whispered, 'I can no longer deny myself you'. After their wild, impassioned embrace, Liszt fell asleep. Even as she looked down at him the thought passed through her mind that she would lose him: 'He was mine; but when he waked he would perhaps recoil from me, and, weeping, take refuge at the feet of a crucifix . . . Yes, I must lose him: on awaking he would seek out some priest or other, and, face in the dust, he would implore God's pardon for the crime of love, which, at the tribunal of penitence, he would sully with names of the most hateful kind.' Taking hold of the poisoned dagger that it was her custom to carry with her, Olga waited for him to stir: 'One tiny puncture, and he was mine to all eternity, for we would lie under the same shroud in the same tomb. I held the dagger in the hollow of my hand and waited for his first word. It was one of love. He was saved.'

Olga followed Liszt to Weimar. There, in the week before Easter, he had a fit of repentance. 'His eyes became veiled, he turned a timid glance towards heaven. He spent the whole of the afternoons of Good Friday and the following day in church: on his knees before the image of Christ he poured forth tears in abundance and smote his breast.' Then suddenly on Easter day, even while the bells were ringing, he burst into her room, a changed man: 'He was radiant. He carried his head proudly. His eyes were ardent, passionate. He embraced me: never did Christian celebrate better the resurrection of his Saviour. "You see, my dear," he said, "there's nothing like putting your conscience in order". I understood then that he was accustomed to these periodic repentances . . . Every six months, in fact, he consecrated a week to the salvation of his soul . . . my heart melted into bitter sadness. This man no doubt believed in the efficacy, in the sight of heaven, of his pitiable trickeries.'

A caricature of the Abbé Liszt, inspired by the second of his 'deux legendes' of 1866: 'St Francois de Paule marchant sur les flots'

From Weimar Olga accompanied Liszt to Hungary, where he was engaged in the setting up of a National School of Music in Budapest. They were joined there by Cardinal Hohenlohe, who was keen to promote the idea. One afternoon when they were left alone together Olga entertained the Cardinal with her racy account of the physical nature of the passion described in *The Song of Songs, which is Solomon's*. Hohenlohe explained that the object of the love so passionately praised in the song was 'the Church and that it should not be so mocked'. But Olga persisted with her ironical comments until Liszt arrived on the scene. 'My dear Abbé,' the Cardinal asked, 'has the Countess ever paraphrased *The Song of Songs* for you? Ask her to do so.' Before he could reply came Olga's thrust, 'Monseigneur, the Abbé prefers the real thing.'

Towards the end of 1870, Olga was informed by her banker that she was ruined. Now she appropriated the legacy that she had settled on her child, but by Easter of the next year this too had been squandered in her desperate efforts to keep a hold on her lover:

He loved luxury; like the artist he was, he could conceive of love only as surrounded by every refinement, every delicacy. He could expand only in rooms lit by alabaster lamps that exhaled perfumes: under his feet he needed soft white carpets: his eyes demanded the satisfaction of rare fantastic shrubs: love, for him, was inseperable from the silks and the finest tissues of all kinds.

It could be a description of Wagner himself, who by this time had made merry with, and finally married, Liszt's daughter Cosima.

One day Olga asked Liszt, 'What would happen to me if I were ruined?'. Quite drily came his reply; 'You would go and take an airing in your own country'. But the end came about in a sorry manner, when Olga made a mess of Chopin's Ballade in G minor at a charity concert. Janka Wohl was present:

On the evening of the concert a brilliant audience assembled. The Countess arrived, on the arm of Liszt, wearing a violet dress buttoned up to the throat. He got her a seat in the little drawing-room, with open colonnades facing the audience, which was reserved for the artists.

When her turn came she was very graciously received, and she commenced her ballad, of course playing by heart. All went well until the sixth page, when she hesitates and gets confused.

In desperation she begins again, encouraged by indulgent applause. But at the very same passage her overwrought nerves betray her again. Pale as a sheet she rises. Then the master, thoroughly irritated, stamps his foot and calls out from where he is sitting: 'Stop where you are!' She sits down again, and, in the midst of a sickening silence, she begins the wretched piece for the third time. Again her obstinate memory deserts her. She makes a desperate effort to remember the final passages, and at last finishes the fatal piece with a clatter of awful discords.

I was never present at a more painful scene. Going out, the master upbraided her more than angrily, as she clung to his arm. He had been severely tried, and he at last lost all patience with the freaks of his pupil. And, this breakdown confirming, as it did, his oft-expressed opinion that she was not of the stuff that artists are made of, he no longer spared her.

The Countess went home, took a dose of laudanum, and slept for forty-eight hours. They thought she was dead.

When she recovered Liszt insisted that she should leave the city immediately. In revenge, she tried to kill both Franz and herself. 'Spare me from having to write of her violence and furies', he wrote in a letter to Carolyne, 'and do me the favour not to talk about her to anyone. My good angel preserved me from danger. After another attempt to poison herself in my room, Madame Janina left for Paris, where she will probably settle.'

But Liszt's desire to hush things up was to be confounded by the fiery Countess herself, for she published two accounts of her affair with Liszt, *Souvenirs d'une Cosaque* and *Souvenirs d'une pianiste*, under the nom-de-plume Robert Franz. Far from being the inventions of a revengeful woman, as they have been discounted by the early biographers, Ernest Newman has shown them to be consistently truthful in point of fact, and penetrating in their insights into Liszt's divided personality.

As Bernhardi had observed, Liszt was 'not a man of transcendent intelligence' but, 'a weak character', easily led by the domineering women he seemed to attract. Olga Janina was a wholly destructive influence, but the two strong-willed women before her, the Countess d'Agoult and the Princess Sayn-Wittgenstein, were ambitious for him, channelled his energies in the right direction, and his life was the more fulfilled for his having found them. They too had observed the disharmonies

Olga Janina (above) the fiery cossack countess who gained access to the Villa d'Este (right and previous pages) by dressing as a garden boy

of his soul: the vanities and the repentances; the tricks of the circus-rider and the devotions of the priest; the love of society and the need for solitude; the success of the performer and the despair of the composer—'Mephistopheles disguised as a Priest'. This duality is the key to the understanding of Liszt as a man, and as an artist.

His private agonies, and the torments of his soul, find expression time and time again in his diaries and other writings. In a letter to the *Gazette Musicale*, shortly after his triumph over Thalberg in 1837, Liszt hinted at the dilemma that confronted him.

The artist is essentially a solitary . . . Though circumstances may throw him into the centre of society, he creates for his own soul, amid these dischordant noises, an impenetrable solitude to which no voice can penetrate. Vanity, ambition, cupidity, jealousy, love itself, all the passions that sway mankind, remain outside the magic circle he has traced about his thought . . . While the entire world is acclaiming the work with enthusiasm, *he* remains only half-satisfied, discontented, and would perhaps destroy it were it not that a new apparition turns his gaze away from what has been accomplished towards those fresh ecstasies of creation.

But in his solitude, away from the applause to which he was by now accustomed, he fell prey to the demon of self doubt:

I feel within myself a deplorable fatigue and a strength more deplorable still, no hope, no desire, a profound 'ennui', too much discouragement or indolence to seek or to avoid anything at all, a body more inured to fatigue than that of a buffalo, a sombre, proud, exasperated soul, a character that is indolent, silent. Please God that my activity may open out some day, even if it be in twenty years. I will wait.

This feeling of impotence was to be perpetually recurrent in him. Though his deeper self despised his easy public success he was always greatly dependent on external stimuli to put him in the mood for sustained composition.

Isolation is bad for me. I feel I have no strength left in me. I live in a state of utter discontent. My past years seem to me so shameful, so pitiable—yet in my solitude I cannot work. My time is almost wasted. I agitate and torment myself in vain.

It was Marie's profound sorrow to see how incapable he was of fighting against that side of his nature that lusted after the world and its cheaper prizes. It hurt her to see him forever writing showy transcriptions of other people's compositions just because the publishers said they were more saleable than his own.

Franz derided these mercantile exigencies or was irritated by them, but in the end he had to submit; and not wishing, as he said, to profane purer art by contact with these commoner things, he abruptly ceased to occupy himself with serious work . . . He put out of sight the compositions of his own that he had sketched. But he could not easily put them out of his mind; and so, in his exasperation, drawn in opposite directions, he sought, in order to escape from himself, distractions in the outer world, whence I used to see him return more and more dissatisfied, more and more out of equilibrium.

The warring elements in him, this lack of equilibrium, gives rise to an agonized outburst in his diary:

There is a storm in the air. My nerves are irritated horribly . . . I feel an eagle's claws tearing at my breast; my tongue is dried up. Two opposed forces are at war within me: one of them impels me towards the immensities of infinite space, high and ever higher beyond all the suns and all the heavens;

The monastery of Sta. Francesca Romana in Rome, one of Liszt's retreats

the other draws me towards the lowest, darkest regions of calm, of death, of annihilation. And I stay nailed to my chair, equally wretched about my strength and my weakness, not knowing what will become of me . . .

And not for the last time did a woman watch his secret struggle with himself, and how it manifested itself in his piano playing. However much he might rail at the vulgarity of the public, as soon as he appeared before it, he became the showman, the virtuoso, anxious to dazzle and be applauded. Still sensitive to her equivocal position as his mistress, Marie used to remain seated behind a screen during a concert. Once on an impulse she moved the screen, and their eyes met:

How can I describe what I felt? It was Franz I saw, and yet it was not Franz. It was as if someone were impersonating him on the stage, with great art and verisimilitude, yet had nothing in common with him except the facial resemblance. And his playing disturbed me. His prodigious, brilliant, incomparable virtuosity was indeed there, there, but I felt it was nevertheless as something alien to me. Where were we? Was I dreaming? Was I a victim of delirium? Who had taken me there and for what purpose? I felt an inexpressible anguish . . .

Yet at the very height of his worldly success —applauded by the crowd, decorated by Princes, adored by women everywhere—the religious side of him was deeply troubled. The disgust set in. He wrote to Marie in 1847:

I have conceived a disgust for my piano . . . I do not know why the crowd listens to me and pays me. The acclamations of the crowd, the intoxications and excesses of my life, and the banal and lying embraces of my mistresses . . . have resounded the pitiless funeral bell of that fatal hour when I left you.

Within a year he had retired for good from the life of the travelling virtuoso. But even in the more settled life at Weimar he was subject to the same fits of indolence and self-doubt, the same passion for worldly distractions. That his twelve years in Weimar were so rich in achievement as composer was in no small measure due to the determination of the Princess Sayn-Wittgenstein. That Carolyne succeeded where Marie had largely failed was simply because Liszt's desire for fame and fortune as a virtuoso pianist had by then been satisfied and she was able by her constant supervision to force him to settle down to

composition, and to keep him at it:

For twelve years in Weimar I had to do my own work in the same room with him, otherwise he would never have composed. It is not genius he lacks, but the capacity to sit still—industry, prolonged application. Unless someone helps him in this respect he is impotent, and when the consciousness of his impotence takes possession of him he has to resort to stimulants. This makes his condition still worse, and so the vicious circle widens.

While in private Liszt was as tormented and divided as ever, in public the actor donned his mask, as the composer Cornelius remarked:

With Liszt one is always uneasily conscious of the mask he puts on for the world. He appears to be all energy and courage: a man of extraordinary goodness of heart, self-sacrificing, full of charity, the high-priest, if ever there was one, of a religion of art. Yet he wants himself, himself and again himself; no doubt about that.

But Liszt knew only too well the essential tragedy of his life—this split in him that so tormented his soul. Laughingly he said one day, 'I am half Zigeuner [gypsy], half Franciscan'. Bernhardi was more direct, 'Half Saint, Half Charlatan'. And Gregorovius echoed him, 'Half priest, half circus-rider'. Cornelius divided him in three, 'A third minstrel, a third chevalier, a third Franciscan'. But Marie in her bitterness could only find to say, 'A charming good-for-nothing, an upstart Don Juan, half-mountebank, half-juggler'.

Few men have had to labour at the wearisome task of self-correction as I have. A gifted man once said to me, not inaptly, 'You really have to deal with three men in you, who run counter with each other—the convivial man of the salons, the virtuoso, and the thoughtful creative artist. If you ever manage to come to terms with one of them, you will be able to congratulate yourself on your luck.'—Well, we shall see, we shall see!

The ability to harmonize these disparate elements of his nature eluded him to the end of his days. He became increasingly disillusioned with his music, more and more swamped by the crowd. And so he laments, 'Believe me I would gladly give up all the applause, all the enthusiasm, if I could only produce one really creative work.' But then he adds, 'If I had only written the "Faust" and the "Dante" Symphonies I shouldn't be able to give my friends trout with iced champagne!'

Chapter 5

'As a Horse to an Arab'

You see my piano is for me what his frigate is to a sailor, or his horse to an Arab—more indeed: it is my very self, my mother tongue, my life. Within its seven octaves it encloses the whole range of an orchestra, and a man's ten fingers have the power to reproduce the harmonies which are created by hundreds of performers.

Franz Liszt

In the first half of the nineteenth century Paris developed as the centre of the musical world, and by the 1830s it had become the Mecca for all the great pianists of the age. Liszt had conquered the *salons* as a child prodigy, and later had returned to share the honours with Chopin.

But there were literally dozens of other virtuosos sharpening their wits or their techniques to win the acclamation of the Paris audience, each with his different style and nearly all with their own speciality in piano technique. Moscheles, the bravura artist in the classical tradition, had once been supreme, then Herz with his rapid finger work, and Henselt who could stretch an easy twelfth in both hands. The virtuoso Kalkbrenner, whose clarity and precision excited the crowd, offered to 'make a pianist of Chopin in three years'. He was 'polished as a billiard ball,' said one observer, and 'controlled his obedient fingers as a captain a company of well-drilled soldiers.'

Typical of the virtuosity of the time was Dreyschock, who specialized in octaves. He would practise them sixteen hours a day until he could play them as rapidly and as smoothly as a normal single-note passage. His most popular stunt was to perform Chopin's great 'Revolutionary' Study playing the formidable left hand part in octaves! Heine once said that when he played his octaves in Munich, you could hear them in Paris if the wind was in the right direction. 'He makes a hell of a racket.' Heine mocked

*Left: Liszt, the new champion
Below: Ignaz Moscheles—
once supreme*

the debut of the 'piano-pounder' in Paris. 'One does not seem to hear one pianist Dreyschock but *drei Schock* (three-score) of pianists. Go hang yourself, Franz Liszt! You are but an ordinary god in comparison with this god of thunder!'

Liszt was altogether something else, 'the real diamond among much that is paste—the real instrumentalist among many charlatans.' An English 'amateur', Henry Chorley, wrote this balanced, critical assessment of Liszt's playing at this period in Paris:

In uniform richness and sweetness of tone he may have been surpassed. His manner of treating the piano—his total indifference to wood and wire in his search for effect, could hardly fail to preclude uniform care and finish. But his varieties of tone are remarkable; and as far as I have gone, unsurpassed. He can make the strings whisper with an aerial delicacy or utter voices as clear and as tiny as the very finest harp notes. Sometimes the thing becomes a trumpet and a sound is extracted from the unwilling strings as piercing and nasal as the tone of a clarion.

With regard to the amount of difficulties vanquished, those who have the least comprehended Liszt's mind have been the most wonder-stricken by his attributes. Rapidity and evenness of finger consistent with the most self-controlling power of stopping or retarding a passage to introduce some freak of ornament, to improvise some *shade* of expression—grasp of intervals the most harrassing and difficult (the brass-chords of many of his arrangements extending over two octaves and yet struck so certainly as almost to lose the effect of arpeggio necessary to their production)—the power of interweaving the richest and most fantastic accompaniments with a steadily moving melody—the maintenance of question and answer among several parts—add to these velocity, fire, poignancy in flights of octaves and in chromatic succession of chords. All these gifts, singly or in combination, are sternly or gamely under command of the moment's poetical imagining.

Having conquered Paris, Liszt promptly left it for the solitude of Switzerland and the company of his Countess. In his absence there stole upon the scene a rival more formidable than all the rest: Sigismond Thalberg.

Thalberg's 'three-handed' effect brought Paris to her feet—quite literally, standing up in their places, craning to see how he did it. By playing a sustained melody with alternating thumbs in the middle register of the keyboard, with showers of spectacular, dancing arpeggios from the fingers on either side it sounded for all the world as if he was possessed of three hands. Chopin was not impressed, but then people were beginning to say that Thalberg's music was superior to his own.

As for Thalberg, he plays excellently, but he is not my man. Younger than I, pleases the ladies, makes potpourris from [Auber's] *La Muette*, gets his soft passages by the pedal, not the hand, takes tenths as easily as I take octaves—has diamond shirt-studs—does not admire Moscheles.

He was the illegitimate son of Count Moritz von Dietrichstein and Baroness von Wetzler, with a polished aristocratic manner to match his pedigree. His personal magnetism appears to have been immense and his calm and dignified attitude at the keyboard was allied to an impeccable finger technique, and a skilful use of the pedals. At his best he was a refined and accomplished artist.

Not only did they judge his music to be superior to Chopin, but the Parisians were openly comparing him with Liszt. The gauntlet was down and Liszt rushed back to Paris to 'assert' himself 'against this upstart Thalberg'. 'I shall put a dash of water in the wine of Monsieur Sigismonde.'

But when Liszt arrived in Paris in December 1836 he found that the usurper had just left in triumph. Though the duel would have to wait until the 'upstart' returned the next spring, Liszt wasted no time in rekindling the enthus-

L'Opera, Paris, where 4000 people came to hear Liszt play

iasms of the Paris audience. Sir Charles Halle was present at the concert given by Hector Berlioz at which he made his reappearance.

Such marvels of executive skill and power I could never have imagined. He was a giant, and Rubinstein spoke the truth when, at the time when his own triumphs were greatest, he said that, in comparison with Liszt, all other pianists were like children. Chopin carried you with him into a dreamland, in which you would have liked to dwell for ever; Liszt was all sunshine and dazzling splendour, subjugating his hearers with a power that none could withstand. For him there were no difficulties of execution, the most incredible seeming child's play under his fingers. One of the transcendent merits of his playing was the crystal-like clearness which never failed for a moment even in the most complicated and, to anybody else, impossible passages; it was as if he had photographed them in their minutest detail upon the ear of the listener. The power he drew from his instrument was such as I have never heard since, but never harsh, never suggesting 'thumping'. His daring

was as extraordinary as his talent. At an orchestral concert given by him and conducted by Berlioz, the 'Marche au Supplice' from the latter's *Symphonie Fantastique*, that most gorgeously instrumented piece, was performed, at the conclusion of which Liszt sat down and played his own arrangement, for the piano alone, of the same movement, with an effect even surpassing that of the full orchestra, and creating an indescribable *furore*. The feat had been duly announced in the programme beforehand, a proof of his indomitable courage.

Liszt's next move was to write a slashing attack on Thalberg's music in the *Gazette Musicale*, followed by a letter to the same *Gazette* justifying himself for having done so.

On my arrival in Paris the talk of the musical world was all about a pianist the like of whom had never been heard before; he was to be the regenerator of the art; both as executant and as composer he had opened out a new path along which we ought to

follow him. . . . I was eager to see and study for myself works so new and so profound, that were to introduce me to a man of genius. I shut myself up for a whole morning to study them conscientiously. The result of this study was diametrically opposed to what I had expected. Only one thing surprised me—the enormous effect produced by works so empty, so mediocre. I came to the conclusion that the execution of the composer must be prodigious; and, my opinion having been formed, I expressed it in the *Gazette Musicale* . . .

What I said, I said with regret, driven to it, so to speak, by the public, which had made it its business to link our names together, to represent us as fighting in the same arena for the same crown . . .

The story of Liszt's dealings with Thalberg, as Newman points out, seem all the more distasteful to us now because it is all so unlike the Liszt of the 'legend', the greater-hearted Liszt of later years. But his crown was threatened, and he evidently responded in the very same way that many a lesser man would have shamed himself by doing.

In one thing he most certainly succeeded, and that was stirring up all the fever and excitement of a gladiatorial contest. Thalberg returned to Paris in the March of 1837 and issued what amounted to an open challenge to Liszt by immediately announcing a concert at the Paris Conservatoire. At it he performed his two most celebrated 'war-horses'; his Fantasia on 'God Save the King', and his Fantasia on Rossini's opera *Moses*. Liszt now heard his rival for the first time—and as for the 'three-handed' effect he declared that 'Thalberg is the only man who plays the violin on the piano!' To which insult Thalberg responded by replying, when asked if he would appear at a joint concert with Liszt: 'No. I do not like to be accompanied!'—the kind of comments that would seem more in keeping today with the world of heavyweight boxing—'On the left hand piano, Ladies and Gentlemen, we have "The Great Ugly Bear"—and on the right, "The Louisville Lip" '.

If the first round seemed to go to Thalberg,

then the second was clearly Liszt's. For a start, whereas Thalberg had given his concert in the hall of the Conservatoire which held an audience of four hundred, Liszt, in characteristic style, hired the Opera House and played before an audience ten times as great. It was a triumph—we have Liszt's word for it.

This evening was magnificent for me. You have never seen me so well understood and so much applauded. The public is certainly veering in our direction. Thalberg was stupified with amazement. He said out loud, before several people, that he had never heard anything like it . . .

Notice of the ultimate contest was issued in the pages of the *Gazette Musicale* on 26 March. Round three was held on 31 March in the *salon* of the Princess Belgiojoso, at a charity concert in aid of the Italian refugees. Tickets were to be had at the record price of 40 francs.

Thalberg played first: once again his 'Moses' Fantasia—a dazzling display that brought his fans to the flutter. How would Liszt reply to that! He sat himself at the piano, passed his hands through the locks of his long hair, then launched himself into his 'Niobe' Fantasia, a newly completed piece that showed off to the full his complete mastery of the ring; fistfuls of notes were brought to the attack, dazzling passage work across the seven octaves, much swaying of the body, now ducking, now weaving, feet alive on the pedals, a little flurry with the left hand, a crash of chords in the right. The delicate, dancing fingers of an artist, and the stamina of an Arab horseman.

Heine left us this report:

I forget what he played but I would swear it was variations upon themes from the Apocalypse. At first I could scarcely make them out, those four mystical beasts; I only heard their voices, especially the roaring of the lion and the croaking of the eagle. But the ox with a book in its mouth was very plain to see. What he played best was the Valley of Jehoshaphat. There were lists as in a tournament, and like spectators around the huge space were crowded the resurrected people, coffin-pale and trembling. First came Satan galloping in the lists, black-besaddled on a milk-white charger; and, riding slowly behind, Death on her pale horse. Last came Christ in golden armour, on a black steed. With his holy lance he first thrust Satan down, then Death—and the beholders rejoiced loudly. Stormy applause greeted Liszt's playing. He left the piano exhausted, bowed to the ladies, and upon the lips of the beauties there was that melancholy-sweet smile.

Sigismond Thalberg, the 'three-handed' marvel

They were in no doubt, these beauties, as to the result, yet all eyes were turned to the referee. How would she score the contest? Now, with the same diplomatic guile that she had used to bring the two gladiators together, the Princess Belgiojoso delivered her verdict. 'Thalberg is the best pianist in the world!' A gasp must have gone round the audience. 'But Liszt,' she exclaimed, 'is unique!'

So crushing, in fact, was Thalberg's defeat that little is heard of him thereafter. Liszt had proved himself to be the king of the keyboard, and though his career as a performing virtuoso was to continue for only a further decade, he was to remain the acknowledged Master for most of the remainder of the century; indeed, his mastery has lived on by reputation into the twentieth century, to overshadow even the very greatest of later generations.

As recordings of his virtuosity are obviously denied us, let us relish a moment longer the discerning judgement of some of his great contemporaries.

Frederick Chopin:

I write to you without knowing what my pen is scribbling, because at this moment Liszt is playing my *études* and transporting me out of my respectable thoughts. I should like to steal from him the way to play my own *études*.

Felix Mendelssohn:

Liszt possesses a certain flexibility and diversity of the fingers and an out and out musical feeling which is not likely to have anywhere its equal. In one word, I have not seen any musician in whom musical feeling ran, as in Liszt, into the very tips of the fingers and there streamed out immediately.

Robert Schumann:

How extraordinarily he plays, and how daringly and madly, and again how tenderly and airily—that I have never heard before! . . . Liszt appears to me every day mightier; today he has again played in such a manner that we all trembled and jubilated . . . I have never found any artist except Paganini to possess in so high a degree as Liszt the power of subjecting, elevating and leading the public.

Clara Wieck, who was later to marry Schumann, showed his *Carnaval* and *Phantasiestücke* to Liszt, who promptly played them at sight in incomparable fashion.

Liszt played at sight what we toil over and at the end get nowhere with . . . I sobbed aloud, it overcame me so. Beside Liszt, other virtuosos appear so small, even Thalberg.

Clara was not alone in being dazzled by Liszt's ability to read at sight. Grieg had listened as Liszt read his A minor Piano Concerto at sight, and was even more astonished at how he read one of his violin sonatas.

. . . in the first place he had never seen nor heard the sonata, and in the second it was a sonata with a violin part, now above, now below, independent of the piano part. And what does Liszt do? He plays the whole thing, root and branch, violin and piano, nay, more, for he played fuller, more broadly. The violin part got its due right in the middle of the piano part. He was literally all over the piano at once, without missing a note, and how he played! With grandeur, beauty, genius, unique comprehension. I think I laughed—laughed like a child.

He sight-read, too, the barely legible manuscript of Mendelssohn's G minor Piano Concerto '. . . in the most perfect manner, better than anyone else could play it'. Ferdinand Hiller had 'long known from experience that Liszt played most things best the first time, because they gave him enough to do'. That also was the great violinist Joachim's experience of Liszt:

Heinrich Heine

What a wonderful experience it was to play sonatas or other chamber works with Liszt for the first time. At the second or third performance, however, Liszt could not refrain from playing quite simple passages in octaves or thirds, converting ordinary trills into sixths, and indulging in fiddle-faddle of this kind even in such a work as the 'Kreutzer' Sonata of Beethoven.

Chopin is also reported to have been upset by the way Liszt constantly embellished other people's music: 'If you cannot play the music as it is written it would be better that you did not play it at all.' So too was Mendelssohn:

Liszt has forfeited a considerable portion of my esteem through the tomfool pranks he has played not only with the public—which doesn't matter—but with the music itself. He performed works by Beethoven, Bach and Handel in such a pitiably imperfect style, so uncleanly, so ignorantly, that I could have listened to many a middling pianist with more pleasure. Here six bars were added, there seven were omitted; here wrong harmonies, there a horrible fortissimo was employed in the softest passages, and there were all sorts of other lamentable misdemeanours.

Left: Robert Schumann, composer and editor of The New Journal of Music, *together with his wife, the pianist Clara Wieck Right: Felix Bartholdy Mendelssohn*

But these misdemeanours must be seen in the context of the times. Concerts, like visits to the opera, were great social occasions and not the solemn affairs they so often are today. It was a brave virtuoso indeed who demanded silence when he played. The men came to be seen, the ladies to show off their fans and their jewels. The patrons would come and go as they pleased, laugh and smoke and eat. Besides, concerts tended to be very long, and were variable in quality and mixed in their fare. A typical Philharmonic concert in London in the 1830s would consist of 'two symphonies, two overtures, besides two grand instrumental and four vocal pieces. I can never enjoy more than half', Moscheles complained.

Rival virtuosi—each with his own special bag of tricks—not only had to vie against each other, but also had to win the attention of the audience. Liszt was supreme on all counts. He was the first to play from memory, and he was the first to give solo recitals, or 'soliloques' as he called them. The first such solo concert was the first to give solo recitals, or 'soliloquies' the Princess Belgiojoso about them:

... these tiresome musical solioquies (I do not know what other name to give these inventions of mine) with which I contrive to gratify the Romans, and which I am quite capable of importing to Paris, so unbounded does my impudence become! Imagine that, wearied with warfare, not being able to put together a programme that would have common sense, I have ventured to give a series of concerts all by myself, affecting the Louis XIV style, and saying cavalierly to the public, *le concert, c'est moi*. For the curiosity of the thing, I copy a programme of my soliloquies for you:
1 Overture to *William Tell*, performed by M. Liszt.
2 Fantasy on reminiscences of *I Puritani*, composed and performed by the above-named.
3 Studies and Fragments, composed and performed by same.
4 Improvisations on a given theme—still by same.

By 1840 the term 'soliloquy' had been replaced by the word 'recital'—'What does he mean? How can one *recite* upon the piano?' The programme of his first London recital was:
   1 Scherzo and Finale of Beethoven's 'Pastoral' Symphony
2&3 *Serenade* and *Ave Maria*, songs by Schubert transcribed by M. Liszt.
   4 *Hexameron*
5&6 *Tarantelles*, and *Galop chromatic*.
And then there would be the spontaneous

improvisations on given themes. Sometimes he would be asked to give a rendering of Milan Cathedral, a train, or the joys of smoking, and he had many an opportunity to display a ready wit. Once asked to improvise upon the question as to whether it was better to remain a bachelor he replied: 'As I can only answer this query by a long pause, I prefer to recall the words of a sage—"whichever conclusion you may come to, whether to marry or remain single, you will always repent it." '

Between pieces he 'would leave the platform and, descending into the body of the room, where the benches were so arranged as to allow free locomotion, would move about his auditors and converse with his friends, with the gracious condescension of a prince, until he felt disposed to return to the piano.'

Amy Fay, who was a pupil long after Liszt had settled down in Weimar, gives a striking picture of the Master in public:

Liszt is the complete actor who intends to carry away the public, who never forgets that he is before it, and who behaves accordingly. He subdues the people to him by the very way he walks on to the stage. He gives his proud head a toss, throws an electric look out of his eagle eye and seats himself at the piano with an air as much as to say 'Now I am going to do what I please with you!' ... Liszt knows well the influence he has on people, for he always fixes his eye on some one of us when he plays, and I believe he tries to wring our hearts ...

Moser instances a piece of the showman's quick thinking:

If the applause after, say, a Beethoven sonata was not as vociferous as usual, he would plunge straight into a quite empty piece in which he could display his diabolic art as a pianist; the applause followed and the honour of the virtuoso was saved.

If the women doted, the men tended to tire of his vulgar excesses. Balzac, taking him as the model for the character of Conti, an Italian singer, in his novel *Beatrix*, went so far as to call him a 'charlatan'. But let us allow Heine to put it all in perspective:

It is significant that no one speaks of him with indifference. A man who lacks positive stature cannot in this world arouse either favourable or antagonistic passions. It takes fire to enkindle men, whether to hate or to love. What speaks most for Liszt is the respect with which even his enemies recognize his personal merits. He is a man of unruly but noble character ...

The truly great musician in Liszt, both performer and composer, emerged after he had forsaken the public stage. The Liszt who played in private was the real man. There is the touching story told by Count Apponyi of how Richard Wagner in his nightshirt had come thundering down the stairs of Villa Wahnfried, had flung his arms around Liszt's neck and sobbing with emotion had thanked him for his wonderful playing of Beethoven's 'Hammerklavier' Sonata. And his pupils in Weimar in the 1870s, if they were lucky enough to get him to play, were treated to his finest performances, intensely musical, and unadorned, of Bach, Beethoven, Chopin, Schumann and Schubert. Amy Fay was one of the fortunate ones:

He must be among artists to unsheathe his sword. When he is with 'swells' he is all grace and polish. He seems only to toy with his genius for their amusement, and is never serious ...

Such is his legend that it has always been tempting to wonder how this virtuoso or that would have compared with Liszt. Those who heard both Liszt and the great Anton Rubinstein gave the palm to Liszt. Some said that Rosenthal and Godowsky exceeded Liszt in certain 'specialized' techniques. And Horowitz?—certainly the most brilliant technique of his day, perhaps more flawless even than Liszt's. It is idle to speculate. What we can be sure about is that as far as sheer technique is concerned Liszt made everything sound easy, as Louis Kentner, one of the fine virtuosi of today and specialist interpreter of Liszt's piano music, has written:

He had boundless confidence in what the piano could do, an incredible fertility in inventing new sound-effects and a pair of hands capable of reproducing without hesitation on the keyboard what flashed through his mind. The word 'transcendental' was so often used by him that there can be no doubt as to what technique, with its connotations of hard-working efficiency, of struggle with some recalcitrant matter, meant to him: nothing at all. He created what seemed to all the world insurmountable difficulties; wrote, in everybody's opinion, unplayable piano music, and then proceeded to demonstrate calmly and negligently that the difficulties did not exist, that everything was not only playable but easy. We of a less naturally gifted generation must be content if we can do justice by hard work to what he created with such ease.

But Liszt's apparent technical 'ease' was in

fact the fruit of a good deal of hard labour. When as a child he had gone to the 'tyrant' Czerny in Vienna, this meticulous pedagogue had found his playing

... completely irregular, careless and confused, and he had so little knowledge of correct fingering that he threw his fingers all over the keyboard in an altogether arbitrary fashion.

Basing his studies round Clementi's formidable set of endurance exercises, *Gradus ad Parnassum*, Czerny, with fanatical thoroughness, set about laying the foundations of Liszt's flawless technique. He found the boy responsive and tireless:

Never before had I so eager, talented or industrious a student. Since I knew from numerous experiences that geniuses whose mental gifts are ahead of their physical strength tend to neglect solid technique, it seemed necessary above all to use the first months to regulate and strengthen his mechanical dexterity in such a way that he could not possibly slide into bad habits in later years.

Then, inspired by Paganini, he had worked 'four or five hours [a day] at exercises (thirds, sixths, octaves, tremolos, repeated notes, cadenzas, etc)'. Wilhelm von Lenz, a pupil in 1828, told of how Liszt used a specially prepared, heavy piano so that 'to play one scale on it is as good as playing ten on another piano'—a device, incidentally, not dissimilar to some of Paganini's finger-strengthening exercises. And throughout his career as a touring virtuoso Liszt used a dumb keyboard which was a permanent fixture in his coach.

Before Liszt, all pianists, with the exception of Beethoven, had employed a basically harpsichord technique, with the fingers curled and the hands as close to the keyboard as possible. Czerny had noted how Liszt had 'thrown' his fingers all over the keyboard, and despite months of Clementi's *Gradus*, which was designed above all to promote complete equality of tone and perfect evenness in all the fingers, Moscheles still noticed many years later all the 'tossing about of his hands', and could never understand how he could accomplish the most perilous jumps with hardly a mishap.

Yet all the freedom he allowed his hands permitted Liszt to *orchestrate*, as it were, on the piano; and the range of his tone colours is remarked on by almost all who heard him. In all branches of technique his 'flying' fingers

Right: Programme for a Liszt recital, or 'soliloquy' as he first called it

Previous pages: Liszt giving a charity concert before Franz Joseph in Budapest, 1872. One of his rare public performances in later life

were master, yet there were some specialized techniques that he made particularly his own. The 'wide skips' as Moscheles remarked, were almost infallible; double chromatic octaves, where the chromatic scale played in octaves is divided between alternate hands (known to this day as 'Liszt Octaves'); rapid repetition of the same note (as in *La Campanella*); and a technique of obtaining a special kind of brilliance in rapid ornamental passages in the higher octaves 'by holding the fingers almost stiffly and not allowing them to move with much independence, and by throwing the hand, as it were, at the passage where it begins'.

So too did he master and extend the technique of the pedals, to enrich the sonority, to blend or blur the harmonies, to soften the percussiveness, or harden it, to sustain the harmonies and set the hands free, to create, even, an 'impressionistic' haze.

His hands, according to Amy Fay, were 'very narrow, with long and slender fingers that look as if they had twice as many joints as other people'. But his stretch, contrary to some testimonies, was not exceptional. Carl Lachmund studied with Liszt in the 1880s and noted:

At the last chord [of the slow movement of the 'Hammerklavier' Sonata of Beethoven] which is

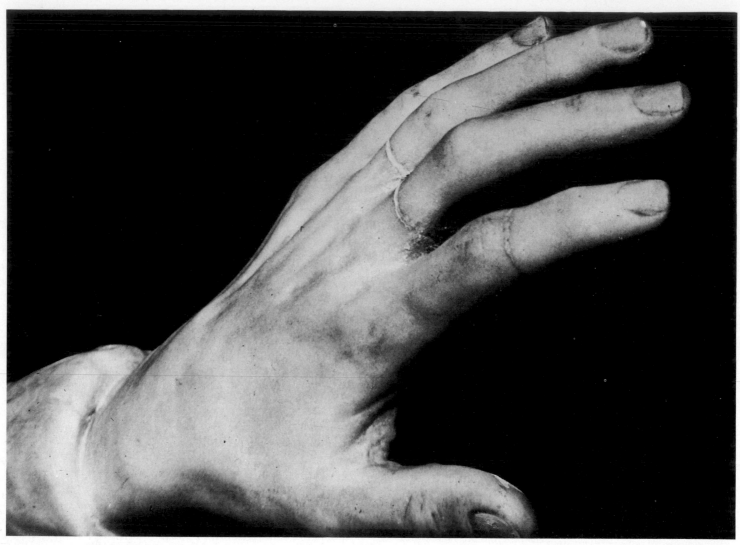

reiterated four times slowly, I was watching his hands, which he usually held in unconventional disregard of rules. It struck me that he could barely cover the tenth in each hand sufficiently to play the chord quietly, without breaking it.

And afterwards Lachmund says that Liszt said to him: 'The public credits me with having a very large hand, but you see I can just stretch this tenth to play it quietly.' Liszt's hands were remarkable, as Louis Kentner has pointed out, 'not so much for their size or length of their fingers as for the low-lying mass of sinews and connective tissue which gave the fingers unusual freedom of movement'.

From his pupils we learn that he used a higher seat than was customary before him, so that the forearm sloped down to the wrist rather than being held horizontally. He played with loose shoulders, a high position of hands, and, so says the redoubtable Amy Fay, with

the hands turned slightly outwards 'so that they naturally covered the E major scale'. The increased height gave him greater weight, and correspondingly more power, though it is often emphasised by those who heard him that Liszt never sacrificed beauty of tone for mere volume of sound; and an otherwise hostile London critic in 1886 wrote that 'his touch is exquisite. Liszt, unlike his pupils, is no piano-smasher. He strokes the keys and seems to "coax" the tone out of them.'

Whilst the beauty of his tone in even the loudest passages is not to be doubted, the pianos of 1886 were much more sturdily constructed than they had been fifty years earlier when Liszt had quite a reputation as a slayer of pianos, as the poet Saphir confirms:

After the concert the victorious chief remains master of the battle field. The conquered pianos

Plaster cast of Liszt's left hand; his fingers had unusual freedom of movement

Previous pages: Liszt as a young man, with two of his mistresses, Charlotte von Hagn and (inset) Lola Montez. The two painted ladies are by Joseph Stieler and hang in The Gallery of Beauties in the Nymphenburg Palace, Munich

64

He appears with the smile of conscious superiority, tempered by the modesty of his garment (as abbé). Tremendous applause.

The first chord—R-r-r-rum!—Looking back, as if to say: 'Attention,—I now begin!'

With eyes closed, as if playing only to himself. Festive vibration of the strings.

Pianissimo. Saint Assisi Liszt speaks to the birds.—His face brightens with holy light.

Hamlet's broodings; Faust's struggles. Deep silence. The very whisper becomes a sigh.

Chopin, George Sand, Reminiscence, Sweet youth, Moonlight, Fragrance and Love.

Dante's Inferno. Wailings of the condemned—(among them those of the piano). Feverish excitement. The tempest closes the gates of hell.—*Boom!*

He has played; not only *for* us but *with* us. Retiring, he bows with lofty humility. Deafening applause. *Eviva!*

Caricatures from a Hungarian paper

lie scattered around him, broken strings float like trophies, wounded instruments flee in all directions, the audience look at one another, dumb with surprise, as after a sudden storm in a serene sky.

The cartoonists had a field day; a staid professor at the Paris Conservatoire 'trembled, not for the pianist but for the piano, expecting to see the strings break at any moment and the hammers fly into splinters'; and when Liszt played Heine felt both blessedness and anxiety, 'but rather more anxiety . . .'

Though by the mid-1830s the piano had evolved mechanically to all extents and purposes into the piano as we know it today, it was nevertheless not strongly enough constructed to withstand the onslaughts of the new breed of virtuosi. The instruments had previously been confined to more intimate

music-making in relatively small rooms; now they were called forth into the concert halls. So fragile were they in fact that Liszt would refuse to take the platform unless there was a spare; sometimes, indeed, there would be three, and Liszt would move from one to another in the course of a performance. Even in the 1870s, when he was teaching in Weimar, he would take delivery of a new Bechstein every year.

The piano was born of the harpsichord in 1709, in Florence. Bartolommeo Cristofori invented it 'to obviate the bad habit of the harpsichord, which could not express colouring at all, or expressed it in exaggerated contrasts by its stops', and he called his new instrument a '*gravicembalo col pian e forte*',—that is a harpsichord, which, because it is struck from underneath the strings by the jack rather than plucked by it, has the ability of producing

65

piano and *forte* by touch alone.

Quickly abandoned in Italy the piano was taken up in Germany—most notably by the great organ builder Gottfried Silbermann—and during the next forty years assumed its square form from the influence of the more prevalent clavichord in Germany. But by the 1760s the piano had once again taken to its 'grand' form at the hands of the famous harpsichord makers in London, Jacob Kirckman and John Broadwood. The piano took even longer to become accepted in Paris and when in the 1780s the famous Pascal Taskin presented one of his new pianos at court he was told, 'Whatever you may do, this newcomer will never oust the majestic harpsichord'. So for the best part of a century the piano remained really just a modified form of harpsichord.

It was not until the last years of the eighteenth century, and then really after 1800, that the piano in its modern form began to emerge from the workshops of Broadwood in London, Sébastian Érard in Paris, John Hawkins in Philadelphia and Alphaeus Babcock in Boston. Many others of course helped it on the way, but these were the great pioneers.

Now, with its single keyboard, the 'pianists' were beginning to demand a great range for their instrument. The five octaves of the harpsichord were increased to six, then six and a half, and finally seven. At the same time strings became heavier and the soundboard correspondingly thicker. Bridge construction had to be modified, and the pitch was raised. With an overall tension now increased to close on twenty tons, the all-wooden frame of the 'harpsichord' construction was no longer adequate. Hawkins, in 1800, inserted metal braces between the wrest-plank and soundboard. In 1808, Broadwood tried to apply tension bars to the treble, but was not wholly successful in fixing them; but in 1821 he further strengthened his construction by extending steel bars over the strings longitudinally, a system which Érard was also to adopt three years later. Broadwood cut away the traditional square sides of the 'harpsichord' so that the keyboard, and hence the virtuoso's hands, could be clearly visible to the audience; and it was he, too, who gave the piano its characteristic two pedals.

To Érard falls the distinction of having invented, in 1821, the 'double-escapement' action, which is the foundation of the action which is still extensively used to this day. The 'double-escapement' made it possible for a note to be repeated without its key having first to return to its position of rest. It was a piano incorporating this new action that Érard gave to the boy Liszt shortly after his arrival in Paris, and it was this instrument that the young virtuoso 'promoted' on his early tours, with his dazzling trick of rapidly repeated notes: a piece such as *La Campanella* was now indeed possible.

Piano makers experimented with all kinds of coverings for their hammers: sheepskin, deer leather, coarse woollen cloth, gutta-pércha, sponge, cork, tinder, even india-rubber. Felt was first patented by Pape, in France in 1826, and by the Universal Exhibition of 1851 felt had become fairly standard. Surprisingly less universal in 1851 was the cast iron frame which had been patented by Babcock in 1825, but it was the cast iron frame that was eventually to solve the problem of the 'piano-smashers'. And it was Babcock again who, in 1830, first patented 'cross-stringing': a new arrangement of the strings in which the treble strings were enabled to fan out over the more resonant central area of the soundboard, with the bass strings crossing them at a slightly higher level. The 'over-strung scale' is more resonant and powerful and a logical development of the piano's move from the drawing room to the concert hall. But it was not until after 1855, when Steinway and Sons of New York had given it its definitive form, that the overstrung scale came into general use.

As the demands of the racing driver benefited the motor car in the twentieth century, so the demands of the concert virtuosi improved the breed of pianos in the nineteenth. Whilst the piano had assumed its basic form by the time Liszt was born, all the most important developments of the instrument took place during the early part of his career. Liszt's natural technique seized on the new possibilities laid open to him, and his fiery imagination, calling as it did on the piano for an ever expanding range of expressions, demanded improvements and refinements from the makers, and above all, a greater strength and reliability. The virtuosi gave the lead; the manufacturers responded, patented their devices and, if they were lucky, turned them into big business.

'Liszt Fantasia' : a caricature from La Vie Parisienne, 3 April 1886

FANTAISIE BRILLANTE SUR LISZT

Chapter 6

Oats For His Horse

Liszt was master of the pianistic effect. As compositions, his passages tend to sound far more difficult than they actually are. The two most outstanding virtuoso-composers, Chopin and Liszt, founded their music on their own experience of the keyboard. Beethoven, though a fine executant himself, set down his notes at the dictates of his mind and not the bidding of his fingers; Schumann, like the Florestan and Eusebius of his character, almost wilfully seems to combine the 'pianistic' with the 'unplayable'; and Schubert composed within his own special technical abilities and limitations, his music rich in chords and repeated octaves and generally lacking in passage work. Chopin, in character with his subdued style of playing, exploits the inherent weakness of the hand, turning it to beautiful account; his music is conceived accordingly, with the comparatively unimportant notes in a passage falling to the weakest fingers. And Liszt, in keeping too with his more flamboyant style of playing, makes much more comprehensive demands in his music.

But if it is true that Chopin's music lies more or less comfortably under the hand, it is even more true of Liszt's. 'In many ways,' writes Louis Kentner, 'Liszt's music is easier to perform than Chopin's because the latter, though he wisely limited himself almost entirely to the piano, nevertheless retained a certain abstract and idiosyncratic quality, a proud insistence that the music comes first and that difficulties simply had to be overcome (a demand Chopin himself was not always able to fulfil), whereas Liszt obviously never wrote anything down that he at least could not play immediately.'

And yet, and yet . . . didn't Robert Schumann describe the twelve *Études d'Exécution Transcendante* as 'studies in storm and dread for, at the most, ten or twelve players in the world'? Schumann was writing of the version published

in 1839. Thirteen years later Liszt revised them, giving them titles, and eliminating some of their most fearsome difficulties. It is in this later version that we usually hear them today; yet even so, with their diabolical octave passages, their wide, unnerving 'skips' and stretches of tenths to be taken at speed, they can only be successfully performed by virtuosi of the highest calibre.

The 1839 version is itself a re-working of his *Études—Opus 1* published in 1827 when he was just sixteen. The Czerny-like study in double thirds (Op 1, No. 4) becomes the wild *Mazeppa*, a study truly of 'storm and dread'.

Feux Follets (No. 5), which follows it, is also clearly derived from the earlier set, but assumes a very much more difficult form:

Liszt: Op. 1, No 5 (1827)

Liszt: *Feux Follets* (1852)

The latter is masterly for its grace and delicacy.

No 7, *Eroica*, No 8, *Wilde Jagd* and No 10 in *F minor*, are all 'storm and dread'; whilst No 3, *Paysage*, No 9, *Ricordanze* and No 11, *Harmonies du Soir* are among the most poetic of his creations.

If the set of Transcendental Studies owes much to the influence of Paganini, the other famous set of Liszt studies was directly inspired by him. In the same year, 1838, Liszt completed his piano transcriptions of five of Paganini's violin *Caprices*, and once again some of the difficulties were so formid-

Drawing by Tobin, from a photograph

able that a revised and simplified edition was presented in 1852. The 1852 version of the E major Study, No 4, for example, has become a more or less straight transfer of Paganini's notes to the keyboard, even confining itself to the violin-like single stave.

Liszt: 'Paganini Study' No 4, 3rd version

Paganini's original:

Paganini: *Caprice* in E major

Liszt's first version of 1838 gave 'spiccato' arpeggios to both hands simultaneously:

Liszt: 'Paganini Study' No 4, 1st version

His second version, also dated 1838, is altogether more formidable with double arpeggios in each hand:

Liszt: 'Paganini Study' No 4, 2nd version

and later in this second version Liszt takes the 'diabolical' liberty of giving triple arpeggios to the right hand, set against a melody in the left:

Liszt: 'Paganini Study' No 4, 2nd version

If the technical difficulties of this last example seem a little extreme, it does show that in the six *Études d'exécution transcendante d'après*

Paganini Liszt was not content with a mere transference of Paganini's notes onto the keyboard. Instead he attempted to recreate the problems that confront the violinist in the original with an equivalent set of keyboard problems for the pianist. In the eighth variation of No 6, for instance, a straight transference of what is a very difficult series of triple stopping for the violin would present no difficulty whatsoever on the piano:

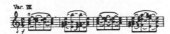

Paganini: *Caprice* No 24, Var. 8

Liszt turns the chords on their heads, expanding the intervals to give a series of widely spaced broken chords to one hand and a series of rapid skips to the other:

Liszt: 'Paganini Study' No 6, Var. 8

In the second study we find an example of the double octaves that Liszt invented as part of his armoury of special tricks, and which are known to this day as 'Liszt Octaves':

Liszt: 'Paganini Study' No 2

Study No 5, *La Chasse*, skilfully recaptures on the piano Paganini's wizardry with harmonics in double stops. No 6 is a set of eleven variations on the theme that Brahms, Rachmaninov, and recently Penderecki, also used.

But the best known of the 'Paganini Studies' is the third of the set, *La Campanella*, which was drawn not from a *Caprice* but from the finale of Paganini's Violin Concerto in B minor. It begins with a series of wide 'skips', one of the hallmarks of Liszt's technique:

Liszt: *La Campanella*, 2nd version

and then becomes a study in rapid note repetition—the virtuoso's tribute to Sébastian Érard's 'double-escapement' action.

Liszt: *La Campanella*, 2nd version

But each study is not confined to just one problem of technique, as were those of say Czerny and Clementi. Chopin's genius had turned the study into a poetic musical expression. Liszt abandoned completely the musical exercise form, and created the 'Concert Study', which combines poetry with display. Such are the three *Études de Concert*, which date from 1849 after Liszt had settled in Weimar. Their titles are *Il Lamento*, *La Leggerezza*, and *Un Sospiro*—each indicative of its character. Chopinesque in style, the last two rank among Liszt's finest work. Nor must one overlook two further concert studies, *Waldesrauchen* which seems to look forward to the world of Ravel, and *Gnomenreigen* which conjures up on the piano the wayward sprites of Berlioz's *Queen Mab* Scherzo and Mendelssohn's *Midsummer Night's Dream*.

If these two are perhaps simpler than the others, then the mighty *Ab-Irato*—subtitled appropriately *Étude de Perfectionnement*—comes as an epilogue to the twelve Transcendental Studies.

Nothing would seem in greater contrast to the *Études* than the three books of lyric pieces known collectively as *Années de pèlerinage*, yet the first two sets were composed during the same period. The *Première Année: Suisse* contains delicate impressions of his first carefree days in the Alps with the Countess D'Agoult. The second piece in the set, *Au Lac de Wallenstadt*, is, in Marie's words, 'a melancholy harmony imitative of the sigh of the waves and the cadence of oars'; a beautiful, evocative piece. *Au bord d'une source* (No 4), forerunner of Ravel's *Jeux d'eau*, is perhaps the best known, and *Les Cloches de Geneve* (No 9) is a lovely nocturne.

The *Seconde Année: Italie* recalls impressions of the year he travelled about Italy with Marie immediately after he had vanquished Thalberg in Paris. In the balm of Marie's

presence, and inspired by the many artistic masterpieces he encountered, he cast aside the external vulgarities of the public virtuoso and plunged deep into creativity. Nearly all the pieces of this collection are directly related to individual works of art: *Sposalizio* with Raphael's painting of the betrothal of the Blessed Virgin in Milan; *Il Penseroso* with Michelangelo's famous statue; and the *Fantasia quasi sonata* '*Après une lecture de Dante*' with Dante's *Divine Comedy* (which he had read, we remember, in the shade of the plane trees of Villa Melzi, and at the foot of Comolli's statue of Dante led by Beatrice), and with his reading of Victor Hugo, from whose poem the title is taken.

The 'Dante' Sonata is one of the most remarkable and impassioned outpourings of all romantic art. The gates of Hell swing back, and with Dante we hear the 'strange tongues, horrible cries', and experience the anguish of the souls who are condemned to inhabit it. Hell-fire is for a moment quenched by a chorale-like melody which is itself transformed into a love duet. Suddenly we are over-whelmed once more by the Inferno. At the end we are allowed just a glimpse of Paradise, before the gates close behind us in a searing

coda. Among the many bold and original is the way Liszt uses the sustaining pedal to suggest the chromatic wailings of the lost souls, and to build them by degrees into the thunderous roar of the flames.

Liszt: 'Dante' Sonata

Later Liszt transcribed three of his songs, settings of Petrarch Sonnets, and these form the central part of this *Second Année*. The 'Petrach' Sonnets in their piano form are among his most beautiful works, the eloquent Sonnet No 104 being the most famous.

But Liszt was unable to sustain such profound creation for long. We have examined in an earlier chapter how the two sides of his nature drew him in opposite directions, how in his solitude he needed the crowd, how the composer needed to become the virtuoso.

Above left: Beethoven their god: Wagner entranced by Liszt's performance of the 'Hammerclavier' (silhouette by Bithorn)
Above: Nicolò Paganini by Ingres

Marie despaired to see him cast aside his own compositions to work on showy transcriptions.

Showy and empty some of these may be, but Liszt was (as the 'Paganini Studies' show) one of the supreme masters of the art of transcription. His contemporaries wrote constantly of the orchestral colours and effects that Liszt was able to obtain on the piano. Never does he merely transfer an orchestral texture to the keyboard, but utilizes his vast experience of keyboard technique to recreate the orchestral sonorities in purely pianistic ways.

The operatic fantasies, rendered unnecessary in this twentieth century of radio, gramophone records, and casettes, were in Liszt's day an important part of the virtuoso's repertoire, and were in great demand among audiences who had very little opportunity to hear the works on the stage. Not only did they fulfil a useful function, but they allowed the virtuosi to display their talents at improvising on well-known melodies. Challenged by Thalberg's *Fantasia on Moses* for example, Liszt had replied with his own *Fantasia on Pacini's 'Niobe'*. They began life as extemporizations and with each repeat performance tended to assume a more definite shape. Eventually they were committed to paper and published as concert Fantasias. There are too many of them (over forty) to do more than make a passing mention of the best: Bellini's *Norma*; Donizetti's *Lucia di Lammermoor*; Gounod's Waltz from 'Faust'; Meyerbeer's *Le Prophète*; Verdi's *Rigoletto* (the quartet) and *Trovatore*; Wagner's *Tristan and Isolda*. Most legendary of all the operatic transcriptions is the *Don Juan Fantasie*, written in 1841. Bernard Shaw described it as 'a work too composite to be described in a single phrase'—so let us let him continue, in his incomparable style:

In so far as it is a transcription it only spoilt Mozart. As a set of variations it is redundant and over-elaborated. But as a Fantasia it has some memorable points. When you hear the terrible progressions of the statue's invitation suddenly echoing through the harmonies accompanying Juan's seductive '*Andiam, andiam, mio bene*', you cannot help accepting it as a stroke of genius—that is if you know your Don Giovanni *au fond*. And the riotous ecstasy of *Finch han dal vino* is translated from song into symphony, from the individual into the abstract, with undeniable insight and power in the finale.

The most notable of the many transcriptions of instrumental pieces (apart from the 'Paganini Studies') are the Berlioz *Symphonie Fantastique*—a performance of which so mesmerized Hallé—and all the nine Symphonies of Beethoven.

The name of Beethoven is sacred in art. His Symphonies are now universally acknowledged to be masterpieces . . . for this reason every way or manner of making them accessible and popular has a certain merit.

But Liszt goes on to

. . . confess that I should have to consider it a rather useless employment of my time, if I had but added one more to the numerous hitherto published piano-arrangements, following in their rut; but I consider my time well employed if I have succeeded in transferring to the piano not only the grand outlines of Beethoven's compositions but also all those numerous fine details and smaller traits that so powerfully contribute to the completion of the ensemble.

Beethoven was to Liszt a god. So much did he respect him that for a long while he refused his publisher's demands to transcribe the great choral movement of the Ninth, as he had, after repeated attempts, become 'distinctly convinced of the impossibility of making any pianoforte arrangement . . . that could in any way be even approximately effective or satisfactory'. Respect for Beethoven's masterpieces is evident in every bar of Liszt's piano transcriptions of them. He did not, of course, just transfer as many of Beethoven's notes as possible onto two staves, as some lesser hacks had done, but came to an understanding of Beethoven's own creative imagination, absorbed every detail, then rethought it in pianistic terms.

In his transcription of Schubert's songs—more than fifty of them, including the two great cycles *Schwanengesang* and *Winterreise*—Liszt also displays a masterly touch. He respected Schubert much as he respected Beethoven, called him in fact 'the most poetical composer who has ever lived'. Once again Liszt does not merely transfer notes, but brings into play his insights as interpreter to fuse the vocal line and the accompaniment into a living entity; a rebirth, so to speak, yet retaining all the character and atmosphere of the originals: the *Erlkönig*, *Ständchen*, *Auf dem Wasser zu singen*, *Meeresstille*, *Gretchen am Spinnrade*, *Der Doppelgänger*—beautifully done, each and every one of them. Schubert was little appreciated outside Vienna at this time and Liszt, by performing his transcriptions, was able to take Schubert's music to a far wider audience.

In 1851 Liszt transcribed Schubert's 'Wanderer' Fantasy for piano and orchestra. The four movements of the Fantasy run without a break and Schubert uses his themes in various forms in all four movements. From this, as Humphrey Searle has pointed out, Liszt derived his idea of 'the transference of themes' as the unifying principle in the construction of his great Piano Sonata in B minor. In it Liszt was consciously striving to create a new sonata form, and it is arguably the finest of all his piano compositions. I stress the 'arguably', for opinion has always been strongly, even passionately, divided on its merits. Nearly every critic attacked it (not an uncommon fate with masterpieces!) and it was spectacularly unsuccessful whenever the composer himself played it—'an invitation to stamping and hissing', so Liszt says in one of his letters. Brahms fell asleep when Liszt played it to him, and it was the beginning of the unpleasant hostility between them. Sacheverell Sitwell, author of the finest Liszt biography in English, whilst admitting it to be 'a proud passage of Romanticism' went on to write that 'In the hands of Busoni, or even Horowitz, it sounds magnificent; but, . . . always empty; and unless it is played by such pianists as these, the awkwardness of the pauses and the jerky, staccato sentiment render the Sonata painful and irritating to the nerves'. The present author is inclined to the alternative view that the Sonata is a master-work. Naturally a good performance enhances all and every piece of music, and it is a prerequisite in a work bristling with technical difficulties and complex thought. In a good performance it does sound magnificent, but not, in my opinion, empty. However one might respond to the sound of the music itself, a brief analysis of its construction might, I hope, guide the ear and help the listener to a greater appreciation of this fine work.

The Sonata lasts for approximately half an hour, without a break, in the manner of Schubert's *Wanderer*, with the traditional four contrasting movements combined into one, and that one constructed in sonata form—Exposition, Development and Recapitulation. The whole work is constructed round just four themes:

Liszt: Piano Sonata in B minor, themes a, b, c and d

The first three of these seemingly incongruous elements are announced immediately by Liszt in a short introduction of only sixteen bars:

Liszt: Piano Sonata in B minor, first 16 bars

Then when the first subject suddenly bursts about us, it is found on examination to be a clever combination of the two elements (b), and (c); notice, too, that the semiquaver passages are also derived from (b):

Piano Sonata; bars 17 and 18 (see marked themes)

Out of the 'storm and dread' of this section and its famous double octaves comes the dark, sinister opening theme (a)

Piano Sonata; reappearance of theme a

Beethoven

which leads to the chorale-like theme (d) of the Grandioso second subject:

Piano Sonata; Grandioso section

Within this second section we come to a beautiful lyrical melody which is a 'transformation' of theme (c).

Piano Sonata; melody in second section

This is restored by what in traditional terms would be the slow movement. Its theme is in fact a 'transformation' of theme (a)—the ominous introduction transformed into one of Liszt's most serene and beautiful passages.

Piano Sonata; andante sostenuto theme

Robert Schumann

The customary Development section is here taken up with a Mephistophelian fugue in three parts, whose subject is clearly derived from a combination of themes (b) and (c):

Piano Sonata; fugue

A little later on the subject is mockingly distorted and turned on its head:

Piano Sonata; fugue subject upside down

The fugue finally leads out of the Development section into the Recapitulation, which begins with a restatement of the first subject and continues with a review of all the main ideas of the Exposition. This culminates in the fearsome octave passage in the coda—itself a 'transformation' of theme (b):

Piano Sonata; prestissimo octaves of coda

This reaches a dramatic climax with the reappearance of the Grandioso theme (d):

Piano Sonata; reappearance of Grandioso theme

The many sudden alterations and contrasts of mood have frequently been explained in terms of Goethe's *Faust*—a work that had an undeniable influence on Liszt—with the first subject portraying Faust, the beautiful theme of the slow movement portraying Gretchen, and the fugue Mephistopheles. Other commentators have explained the contrasts by suggesting that the work is autobiographical and reflects the contradictions in Liszt's own divided character. But there is, I believe, a third and more powerful influence at work—'the sudden contrasts of 'late' Beethoven. Liszt was consciously searching for a new approach to the problem of sonata form; it would be in character for him to explore along the lines indicated by the late masterpieces of the composer whom he venerated above all others, and who had given the sonata form its highest expression.

Another composer whose art Liszt revered was of course Chopin; though since 1840, when Liszt had abused Chopin's hospitality by conducting an affair with the pianiste Camille Pleyel in his apartment, their friendship had cooled. In October 1849, the same month in which Chopin died, and a few days after learning of his death, Liszt composed *Les Funerailles*, ostensibly in memory of Hungarian friends who died in the bloody revolution of the previous year. But the strong similarity between the middle section of *Funerailles* and the central episode of Chopin's famous Polonaise in A flat leaves one in little doubt that he was deeply moved by the death of his former friend.

Chopin: *Polonaise* in A flat

Liszt: *Funerailles*

Funerailles was published as No 7 of the set of pieces called *Harmonies poétiques et religieuses*. The other great work in this collection is *Bénédiction de Dieu dans la Solitude*. Based on a poem of Lamartine and prefaced by a quotation from him, 'Whence comes, O God, this peace that overwhelms me? Whence comes this faith with which my heart overflows?', *Bénédiction* is one of the most moving pieces he ever wrote, a true masterpiece.

To return, for a moment, to the event of Chopin's death—during his life Liszt made no attempt to use the forms that Chopin had made so popular: after his death Liszt tried to make these forms his own. Alan Walker regards this as 'an unconscious symptom of his posthumous identification with Chopin', and continues to point out that 'Liszt's *Berceuse*, for instance, is so closely modelled on Chopin's as almost to constitute a deliberate parody of it'. The key of D flat major is common to them both, the themes of both are similar, and are elaborated with chromatic thirds and Liszt sustains the tonic pedal throughout the entire piece almost in the precise manner of Chopin. It is nevertheless an exquisite piece. Other Chopin forms that Liszt uses are the Polonaise, the Mazurka, the Tarantella and the Ballade. The second of his Ballades, that in B minor, is an especially fine work.

Like Chopin, Liszt now looked over his shoulder towards the music of his native country. He had grown up near the gypsy encampments around Raiding, and on his concert tours of Hungary he had made a special point of revisiting them—he writes most vividly about them in his book on gypsy music. His fifteen *Hungarian Rhapsodies* embody all the danger, colour and gaudy excitement of his experiences with them. In form they are free improvisations or fantasies, based on the two extreme contrasting moods of gypsy music: the *lassau*, slow, irregular in its rhythms and often of a haunting sadness; the *frisa*, very fast and gay, often working up to the very heights of frenzy. The second and Twelfth *Rhapsodies* are colourful, noisy and of immediate appeal; the Ninth, called *Pester Karneval*, is remarkably modern in many of its sounds; the Tenth is celebrated for its *glissandi*; and the Fifteenth is the well-known *Rákoczy March*. The freaks of the gypsy violinists and the native cymbalon are often suggested. Brash and vulgar as they are, the *Rhapsodies* are frequently dismissed as shallow, formless, and little to do with real gypsy music. But they have kept their appeal for more than a century, and they have made the native music of Hungary known throughout the world. But this is what Bela Bartok had to say about them:

The Hungarian Rhapsodies, which should say the most to us, are his least successful works (perhaps that is why they are so generally known and admired). Alongside strokes of genius we find altogether too conventional ideas—gypsy music, sometimes mixed up with Italianisms (No 6), sometimes in complete formal confusion (No 12).

In one or two of the piano pieces composed towards the end of his life Liszt seemed to look forward to, to anticipate, Bartok—as well as several other important future composers. But this must wait until the final chapter.

Before passing from the piano works to those for orchestra there is one other branch of Liszt's writing for keyboard that should not be overlooked: that is his compositions for organ. He wrote very few works for this medium, and most of these few were transcriptions of, or fantasias upon, other peoples' music. George Sand and Adolphe Pictet were never to forget his improvisation on the *Dies Irae* that day in 1836 in the church of St Nicholas in Fribourg. Nor I think, once heard, could anyone forget the two major organ works that he committed to paper: the *Ad Nos ad Salutarem Undam*, a Fantasia and Fugue based on the Chorale from Meyerbeer's *Le Prophète*, a truly magnificent large-scale work which exploits every conceivable resource of the organ; and the Prelude and Fugue on the *name* B.A.C.H.'. These two works alone establish Liszt as one of the few great composers for the organ. After Bach, and before Max Reger, Liszt has no equal.

Right: Béla Bartók

76

Chapter 7

Cavalry

Liszt abandoned his sensational career as a virtuoso pianist in 1847, at the age of only thirty-five, and made his home in Weimar where the two great german poets Schiller and Goethe had both been active. Henceforth he was never again to play the piano for money. His main reason for deciding to settle there was the availabilty of an orchestra, which for at least three months of each year was to be entirely at his disposal. For years he had been content to 'orchestrate' upon the piano, but now the temptation to have the real thing, as well as the fatigue brought on by his travels, led him to accept the post of Honorary Kappelmeister at the Grand-Ducal Court.

A year later, as we have seen, he was taken in hand by the formidable Princess von Sayn-Wittgenstein. The twelve years that he remained in Weimar find Liszt at his most prolific and generally at the very height of his creative powers. Apart from the piano music discussed in the previous chapter, Liszt completed during these years the first twelve of his Symphonic Poems, the 'Faust' and the 'Dante' Symphonies, two Piano Concertos and *Totentanz*.

Liszt had first been associated with the orchestra in Weimar in 1843 and had returned for a short while each season to conduct it. In 1843 the forces at his disposal in the opera-house amounted to an orchestra of thirty-five, a chorus of twenty-three and a ballet of four. The standard, it seems, was not high and Berlioz described the chorus that year as 'a lot of wretches squalling out of tune and out of time'. But by the end of 1851 the standards had greatly improved, and the forces increased: the ballet now numbered seven, the chorus had grown to twenty-nine, and the orchestra had swelled to a grand total of forty-two players:

5 first violins	2 flutes	4 horns
6 second violins	2 oboes	2 trumpets
3 violas	2 clarinets	3 trombones
4 cellos	2 bassoons	1 tuba
3 double basses		

1 harp
1 timpany
1 percussion.
and an organ.

The leader was the young Joachim.

Liszt's earliest essays in the orchestral medium were tentative and for the most part unsuccessful, as the Fantasia on Berlioz's *Lelio* and the 'Malédiction' Concerto (both of the 1830s) bear witness. In the 1840s Liszt received help with his orchestrations from a well-known composer of operettas of the time, August Conradi, who was competent but not imaginative. When Liszt settled in Weimar, Conradi came to join him. In 1849 his place was taken by a younger and far more imaginative composer, Joachim Raff. In his book, *The Music of Liszt*, Humphrey Searle showed how the collaboration process worked with respect to the symphonic poem *Tasso*. The schedule of events was as follows:

August 1 1849	Liszt completes the music in short score on four staves, giving indications of the instrumentation he had in mind.
August 28 1849	The first performance was given of the full score completed by Conradi.
February 19 1850	The second performance given from the score revised by Liszt.
July 1851	The work was tried out in rehearsal in a new version, this time by Raff, but with alterations by Liszt.
1854	Liszt completely revised it, adding a middle section—in which form it is known today.

How lucky Liszt was, as a composer, to have an orchestra ready at his beck and call to try

out the various revisions of his work.

As composer of music for the piano Liszt spoke with the natural authority of one who was master of the keyboard. Now in Weimar as conductor, he gradually gained a mastery of the orchestra through practical experience. By 1854 he had confidence enough to dispense with his collaborators.

Liszt's main orchestral form was the 'Symphonic Poem'—a form which he himself created; its invention is a landmark in the history of music, to be followed in kind, though not in precise style, by Richard Strauss and Sibelius among others. Liszt was preoccupied by what is generally known today as 'programme' music. Often he took as his inspiration a literary subject, or a painting. But he was not concerned to tell a story or to depict a scene; rather he was seeking to express the mood that a particular painting or poem evoked in him; or else he attempted to elucidate some psychological or philosophical problem that concerned him in the language of music. As if to answer an attack on the merits of programme music Liszt wrote:

It is obvious that the things which can appear only objectively to perception can in no way furnish connecting points to music; the poorest of apprentice landscape painters could give with a few more chalk strokes a much more faithful picture than a musician operating with all the resources of the best orchestra. But if these same things are subjectivized to dreaming, to contemplation, to emotional uplift, have they not a peculiar kinship with music; and should not music be able to translate them into its mysterious language?

The twelve symphonic poems composed in Weimar (a thirteenth was published in 1883) have the following titles, which show well their literary background.

1 *Ce qu'on entend sur la montagne*
2 *Tasso. Lamento e Trionfo*
3 *Les Préludes*
4 *Orpheus*
5 *Prometheus*
6 *Mazeppa*
7 *Festklänge*
8 *Héroïde Funèbre*
9 *Hungaria*
10 *Hamlet*
11 *Hunnenschlacht*
12 *Die Ideale*

Overleaf: Pastel sketch of Liszt by Franz von Lenbach and an anonymous bronze relief of about 1890

Tasso was originally written as an overture to Goethe's play 'Torquato Tasso'. In the preface to his revised version of 1854 Liszt wrote that he saw Tasso (the Italian poet) as 'the genius who is misjudged by his contemporaries and surrounded with a radiant halo by posterity'. This is the philosophical problem that obsessed Liszt (especially in later years).

Les Préludes is by far the best known of all the symphonic poems. It is described as being 'after Lamartine'; the preface to it begins with some lines from one of Lamartine's *Méditations poétiques*: 'What is our life but a series of preludes to that unknown song of which the first solemn note is sounded by death?'

Orpheus was written as an introduction to a Weimar performance of Gluck's opera of the same title. This work was considered by Wagner to be Liszt's finest composition, and it is certainly one of the best of the symphonic poems. There is no real programme to it, though in the preface to it Liszt wrote that he had been inspired by an Etruscan vase in the Louvre.

Mazeppa is an impassioned account of Victor Hugo's ballad: it tells the story of Ivan Mazeppa, who was bound naked to a wild horse after having an affair with a young countess. Rescued by the Cossacks, he became their leader in battle against Peter the Great, and afterwards committed suicide. It is all 'storm and dread' like the fourth *Transcendental Study* that bears the same title.

Hamlet is perhaps the finest of all the symphonic poems, a truly remarkable character study in music of the Prince in Shakespeare's play: full of brooding uncertainty and outbursts of violence typical of the melancholic.

Die Ideale is a large-scale episodic work based on a poem by Schiller, the three sections evoking three aspects of the artist's soul: 'Disillusion'—'Now all ideals and hopes have vanished'; 'Aspiration' and 'Creation', in which Liszt repeats the motifs of the first movement 'joyously and assertively as an apotheosis'.

The last of his symphonic poems Liszt composed in the final years of his life, in 1882, when he himself was disillusioned, and it is completely different from the others in style. *Von der Wiege bis zum Grabe* ('From the Cradle to the Grave') has three short distinctive movements: 'The Cradle'; 'The Struggle for Existence' and 'To the Grave, the Cradle of the Future Life'. Gone now are all traces of

display for its own sake; this work is remarkable for its brevity, sparseness of texture, clarity, and concentration of thought.

Liszt's orchestral masterpiece is undoubtedly the hour-long 'Faust' Symphony, composed in just two months in the late summer of 1854. Liszt however constantly revised it, adding to the original scoring (which was for small orchestra) three trumpets, three trombones, harp, organ and percussion. In 1857 he added a final chorus, and revisions continued right up to the 1880s when he added a few bars to the slow movement. The full title hints at the underlying 'programme': 'A Faust Symphony in three character sketches (after Goethe): 1 Faust; 2 Gretchen; 3 Mephistopheles'.

The first movement is generally accepted to be a self-portrait of Liszt, for he is known to have closely identified himself with the character of Faust. Perhaps that is why he hesitated so before writing it and it explains the line in his letter to the Princess earlier in 1854: 'Anything to do with Goethe is dangerous for me to handle'. The biographer Peter Raabe was in no doubt as to the connection between Liszt and Faust:

The brooding protagonist whom he has drawn with such uncanny certainty in the first movement, the ardent lover, the aspirant towards the ideal, who again and again sinks back into darkness when victory seems at hand, is Liszt himself.

It is then of more than passing interest to read Liszt's thoughts on the character of Faust (in this letter of 1869 which compares Faust with Manfred), for it reveals perhaps what Liszt thought of himself:

Faust ... seemed to me a decidedly bourgeois character. For that reason he becomes more varied, more complete, richer, more communicative (than Manfred) ... Faust's personality scatters and dissipates itself; he takes no action, lets himself be driven, hesitates, experiments, loses his way, considers, bargains, and is only interested in his own little happiness.

More than a hint of auto-biography in that.

The tender Gretchen, murmuring her 'He loves me—he loves me not—he loves me!', is portrayed with great delicacy, her theme being given to a solo oboe accompanied by a solo viola.

The evil genius of Mephistopheles is ingeniously portrayed in music by a 'trans-

Right: *Faust, Gretchen and Mephistopheles; from a drawing by Delacroix*

formation' of the Faust themes from the first movement. As Humphrey Searle so succinctly puts it: 'Mephistopheles is the spirit of negation; he can only destroy, not create . . . [He] takes possession, as it were, of Faust, whose leading themes now appear distorted and cruelly misshapen'.

With the 'Faust' Symphony Liszt had by no means finished with the Faust story. In 1860 he composed 'Two Episodes from Lennau's Faust—*Night Ride* and *Dance in the Village Inn*'. Both are wonderful essays in programme music: the first, strange melancholy music, evokes a funeral cortège passing through a forest on a dark stormy night; the second depicts Mephisto seizing the violin and playing a waltz in the village inn. This latter was later transcribed by Liszt for the piano as the first of the four 'Mephisto' Waltzes, and in this form has become one of Liszt's most famous compositions.

The 'Dante' Symphony is Liszt's other great orchestral work. Like the 'Faust' Symphony it is a large-scale work, its two movements lasting for three-quarters of an hour. Like the earlier 'Dante' Sonata, the work was inspired by Dante's *Divine Comedy*; but unlike the earlier piece the Symphony confines itself to the first two of Dante's books, 'Inferno' and 'Purgatory', following Wagner's advice that no music could properly express the joys of 'Paradise'.

Abandon hope, all ye that enter here.

is the theme of the first movement:

Through me is the way to the city of weeping;
Through me is the way to eternal torment;
Through me is the way among those that are lost . . .

Then, in this first movement, Liszt tells of the plight of the illicit lovers, Paolo and Francesca, who could never escape the violent and incessant winds that blew them hither and thither round the second circle of Hell.

Leaving the storms of Hell behind them, the tormented souls now arrive in 'Purgatory', and their yearning for Paradise and the trials that they must undergo to reach it form the subject of the second movement. The work ends with a women's chorus singing the Magnificat, Liszt's solution to the musically unattainable 'Paradise'. Together with the 'Faust' Symphony this work sets the seal on Liszt's greatness as an orchestral composer.

Of his music for piano and orchestra, the Piano Concerto No 1 in E Flat major is the most flamboyant, and hence the most popular; the Piano Concerto No 2 in A major is the most poetic; and *Totentanz* by far the best. This latter, a set of variations on the *Dies Irae* inspired by Orcagna's disturbing fresco 'The Triumph of Death', is a work of considerable power and great richness of imagination. Bartok, whilst evidently annoyed by a short outburst of emotionalism, was an ardent admirer of this fine work:

This composition, which is simply a set of variations on the Gregorian melody 'Dies Irae', is startlingly harsh from beginning to end. But what do we find in the middle section? A variation hardly eight bars long, of almost Italianate emotionalism. Here Liszt obviously intended to relieve the overwhelming austerity and darkness with a ray of hope. The work as a whole always has a profound effect upon me, but this short section sticks out so from the unified style of the rest that I have never been able to feel that it is appropriate . . .

In terms of public regard Liszt, it has always seemed to me, has suffered as a composer on two counts. He has been popular with one section of the public who have responded to the brash, and sometimes vulgar, displays of virtuosity and overlooked the beauties of his (slightly) less accessible works. The other section has been put off his music altogether by these lapses into the vulgar, or 'Italianate emotionalism' as Bartok calls it. Both are the poorer, for Liszt has composed music for both piano and orchestra of the highest order, which displays a rich imagination and an original personality.

Chapter 8

The Champion

But Liszt was no despotic general deploying his cavalry solely to achieve his own personal ends. If the slant of the previous chapter suggests that he used his orchestra as a kind of private tool to further his own discoveries of the orchestra, then this injustice must quickly be put to rights. Liszt was a selfless champion of other men's work.

His ideal was to make Weimar the capital of all the arts, with music taking her place alongside painting, literature and the theatre: '. . . to take as the Alpha and Omega of their endeavour the triple result of a Court as charming, as brilliant, as attractive as possible; a theatre and a literature that neither rots in the top of the granary nor drowns in the cellar; and finally a University. Court—Theatre—University—that is the grand trilogy for a state like Weimar, which can never be of any importance as regards its commerce, its industry, its army or its navy'. But there were neither painters nor poets to take their place alongside the flood of great composers. The art of music was at its zenith.

Renouncing the role of solo pianist and taking his place at the conductor's desk, Liszt became the first of the new race of great conductors. With a permanent orchestra under his command, he set new standards of discipline and performance and laid the foundation of the modern orchestra as we think of it today. His clearly defined artistic policy of promoting and nurturing contemporary talent soon made Weimar into the centre of the new German Music.

His achievements are impressive. In the concert hall he gave the Symphonies of Schumann and Mendelssohn as well as all of the Symphonies of Beethoven, including the Ninth. Oratorios that he conducted included Handel's *Messiah* and *Samson*. He devoted a whole week to Berlioz with performances of the *Symphonie Fantastique*, the *Damnation of*

Faust, *Harold in Italy*, *Romeo and Juliet* and *Benvenuto Cellini*, as well as the overtures to *King Lear* and the *Corsair*.

In the opera house he produced Schumann's *Paradise and the Péri* and *Geneviève*, Beethoven's *Fidelio*, Mozart's *Magic Flute* and *Don Giovanni*, four Gluck operas—*Orpheus*, *Iphigenia*, *Armida*, and *Alceste*, Rossini's *Le Comte Ory*, *La Gazza Ladra* and *L'Italiana in Algeri*, Verdi's *Ernani*, operas by Hérold and Halévy, by Cherubini and Spontini, by Donizetti and Bellini.

But his greatest glory was his association with Wagner. Liszt recognized that Wagner's genius dwarfed his own and he pledged himself to do all in his power to further his artistic aims. The two had first met in Paris in 1840, at a time when Wagner felt scorned, and envied the other's popular success and lavish style of living; and again in 1844 in Dresden, when Liszt offended by flaunting himself backstage with the notorious Lola Montez. But Liszt spoke well of *Rienzi* and Wagner warmed to him, though it was not until four years later that the friendship caught fire. In 1848 Liszt made a special journey to Dresden to see the creator of *Tannhäuser*. The next year, after the Dresden uprising, with a warrant out for his arrest, Wagner escaped to Weimar where Liszt gave the outlaw shelter in the Altenburg. He arrived at an auspicious time. 'The very day when my personal danger became a certainty,' Wagner wrote, 'I saw Liszt conducting a rehearsal of my *Tannhäuser*, and was astonished at recognizing my second self in his achievement. What I had felt in composing the music, he felt in performing it; what I wanted to express in writing it down, he proclaimed in making it sound. Strange to say, through the love of this rarest friend, I gained, at the moment of becoming homeless, a real home for my art . . .'

Wagner missed the actual performance

Left: Franz Liszt by Lenbach

Piano—forte!

because it was not safe for him to appear in public. Afterwards Liszt planned his escape route to Paris via Switzerland, and gave him money for the first part of the journey. From Paris, he wrote to Liszt imploring him to give the first performance of *Lohengrin*. 'You are the only man to whom I would address this request. To no one but you would I entrust the creation of this opera; but to you I deliver it unconditionally, joyfully, calmly.' Wagner was not on hand to be consulted during the preparation and rehearsals but was ecstatic with the result: 'Errors and misconceptions impeded the desired success. What was to be done to supply what was wanted, so as to further the true understanding on all sides, and with it the ultimate success of the work? Liszt saw it at once, and did it. He gave to the public his own impression of the work in a manner the convincing eloquence and over-powering efficiency of which remain unequalled. Success was his reward, and with his success he now approaches me, saying: "Behold, we have come so far; now create us a new work that we may go still further." ' And now that *Lohengrin* had been brought into the world to his satisfaction, Wagner promised, 'I will complete my *Siegfried*, but *only for you* and for Weimar'.

Liszt added *The Flying Dutchman* to the list of his productions, and by the time the two men eventually met again in 1853, Wagner was more-or-less established as the greatest opera composer of his time. 'I regard you as the creator of my present position,' he wrote to Liszt. 'When I compose and orchestrate I always think of you.' How well might he say that. Musical scholars have often pointed out similarities between Liszt's and Wagner's music.

In 1845 Liszt composed a love-song, *Ich möchte hingehn*, which contains the haunting phrase:

a Liszt: *Ich möchte hingehn*

which more than ten years later becomes *Tristan*'s love-motif:

b Wagner: *Tristan*, love-motif

Again there is an obvious similarity between the second act of Wagner's *Walküre* and the main theme of the '*Faust*' Symphony, which Liszt had earlier played to Wagner.

c Wagner: *Walküre*, 2nd Act

Liszt: 'Faust' theme

And on the manuscript of his *Am Grabe Richard Wagner*, composed in memory of his friend, Liszt wrote; 'Wagner once reminded me of the likeness between his *Parsifal* motif and my previously written *Excelsior!*'

e Liszt: *Exelsior*

f Wagner: *Parsifal*

Admit it in private he might, but Wagner was less generous in public. Wagner complained in a letter to Bulow in 1859:

There are many matters on which we are quite frank among ourselves (for instance, that since my acquaintance with Liszt's compositions my treatment of harmony has become very different from what it was formerly), but it is indiscreet, to say the least, of friend Pohl to babble this secret to the whole world.

Liszt's friendship with Wagner in the end undermined his position in Weimar. The Court, though it turned a blind eye to it in

Peter Cornelius, composer and diarist

public, was less than happy to be associated with a man regarded by its neighbours as a dangerous revolutionary. The cost of the Wagner productions led to curbs on music productions in general, and Liszt found himself increasingly obstructed by the manager of the opera-house. And when, in 1858, at the first performance of Cornelius's opera *Barber of Bagdad*, Liszt himself was hissed, he threw in the towel and handed in his resignation, sacrificing his dream of staging the *Ring* in Weimar. He made a last effort to have *Tristan* performed, but to no avail.

There is in the will that he wrote in those sad days a moving passage about Wagner:

His genius has been a torch to me; I have followed it, and my friendship for Wagner has retained all the character of a noble passion. At one time (some ten years ago), I dreamed of a new epoch for Weimar comparable to that of Karl August, an epoch of which Wagner and I were to be the coryphaei, as Goethe and Schiller once were. The meanness, not to say the villainy, of certain local circumstances, all sorts of jealousies and absurdities elsewhere as well as here, have prevented the realization of this dream which would have redounded to the honour of the present Grand Duke. This notwithstanding, I retain the same feeling, preserve the same conviction, which it was all too easy to make evident to everyone. And I beg Carolyne to assent to this by continuing after my death our affectionate relations with Wagner. Who better than she can understand the lofty impulse so resolutely communicated to art by Wagner, his divine sentiment of love and poetry?

But it was Carolyne who drove the wedge between the two men. She did not like Wagner and considered his music to be inferior to her lover's—that and Wagner's incessant demands for money. Though their friendship cooled Liszt always retained a whole-hearted admiration for his friend. In the early years Liszt was as important to Wagner's progress as King Ludwig II was about to become, and when he heard of Wagner's royal bonanza in 1864 he wrote to Carolyne: 'Let us return to Wagner, whom I have called The Glorious. Actually, there can be nothing changed between us. The great good luck, which he has at last encountered, will soften as much as possible a few asperities in his character.'

'. . . a few asperities . . .'—that is good! Liszt did not know yet of Wagner's secret liason with his daughter Cosima, who was married already to Hans von Bülow his favourite pupil. The scandal broke in 1865. Wagner was hounded out of Munich and took refuge in the villa Triebschen near Lucerne. When Cosima gave birth to the first of her children by Wagner, in 1867, Liszt descended on Triebschen to have the matter out. 'It was as if I had seen Napoleon at St. Helena,' he said afterwards. They had no further dealings with each other for the next five years.

Liszt at the villa Wahnfried with Richard Wagner and Cosima

Chapter 9

'The Master Comes'

Once Liszt had left Weimar, of course, they began to miss him. The Grand Duke wanted him back and tactfully suggested that he might like to establish there an international school of pianism. In 1869 Liszt accepted the invitation and taught in Weimar for three months in the early summer for the remaining seventeen years of his life.

Everything was done to make him comfortable. The Court Gardener's House, the Hofgärtnerei, was put at his disposal, and the Grand Duchess herself saw that the decorations and furnishings were carried out to Liszt's taste. 'The walls are pale grey, with a gilded border running round the [music] room, or rather two rooms, which are divided, but not separated, by crimson curtains. The furniture is crimson, and everything is so *comfortable*', wrote the delectable and admiring Amy Fay from Chicago. 'A splendid grand piano stands in one window (he receives a new one every year). The other window is always wide open, and looks out on the park. There is a dovecot just opposite the window, and the doves promenade up and down on the roof of it . . . and sometimes whirr down on the sill itself. That pleases Liszt. His writing table is beautifully fitted up with things that all match. Everything is in bronze; inkstand, paperweight, matchbox, etc., and there is always a lighted candle standing on it by which he and the gentlemen can light their cigars.' The Hofgärtenerie was ideal for his needs. Not too big; four rooms on two floors, and surrounded on three sides by quiet secluded gardens. The music room, on the first floor, was spacious enough not only to take the full-size grand piano but to accommodate thirty or more students.
Liszt gave himself unsparingly to his pupils. He turned no one away and charged nothing for his lessons. Nearly five hundred pianists could boast the claim to be a 'Pupil of Liszt',

Hans von Bülow, who cleaned out the Augean stables

though many of them played to him only once, and at any one time there might be up to fifty clamouring for his attention. In fact the noise of their playing so upset the local inhabitants that there were restrictions on the times of day that they were allowed to practise, and a byelaw was passed forbidding the playing of the piano with the windows open.

They came, these pupils, from America, Russia and all parts of Europe with letters of introduction from Kings and Princesses and famous musicians. They would present their 'passports' to Liszt in private and then be invited to join in the next day in the established routine.

On Sundays they would assemble in the Hofgärtenerei from eleven till one o'clock, for a kind of informal reception which the Grand Duke himself often attended. There would usually be some chamber music, and if Liszt was in the mood he would play himself. These were occasions to treasure, for in the last years of his life he played less and less frequently in public, and never if asked. And gone were the bravura displays of the showman. Only the music mattered now.

On three afternoons a week Liszt held master-classes from four until six. No one dared be late. The students would assemble well before the appointed hour, place their chosen music on the table by the door, and sit quietly until an excited whisper heralded his imminent arrival: 'The Master comes!' Liszt would make his regal entrance precisely on the hour. Everyone would stand; the ladies kissed his hand and their hero bowed like a king. 'He is just like a monarch', observed Amy Fay, 'and no one dares to speak to him until he addresses one first, which I think no fun.' The Master would then say a few words (in French, for he never grew to like the German language), then glance over the music upon the table by the door until some work or other caught his eye. 'Who plays this?' he would ask and the chosen one would take his place at the piano and play with Liszt standing by his side. He would give a running commentary during the performance, stopping the student from time to time to demonstrate a passage or to tell some anecdote about how he himself had played it to the composer. Amy Fay gives an idea of the highly charged atmosphere at these classes:

Today I am more dead than alive as we had a lesson from him yesterday that lasted four hours. There were twenty artists present, all of whom were anxious to play, and as he was in high good-humour, he played ever so much himself in between ... It is a fearful day's work every time I go to him. First, four hours practice in the morning. Then a nervous feeling that takes away my appetite and prevents me from eating my dinner. And then several hours at Liszt's where all sorts of tremendous things are played. You never know before whom you must play there, for it is the musical headquarters of the world.

Liszt was not in the least concerned with technique. He expected his pupils to have already the necessary equipment or to acquire it for themselves. As far as he himself was concerned no practical problems existed and so he did not interest himself in them. 'Do you think I care how fast you can play octaves?' he deflated a student who was showing off, and many a slovenly performer was dismissed with 'We don't wash our dirty linen here!'

'He doesn't tell you anything about technique. *That* you must work out for yourself', declared Amy Fay. But if you were sharp enough you could learn from his example, as Stavenhagen pointed out: 'If one is attentive one can learn enormously from him in technical matters. One must be swift to seize on the Master's technical secrets.'

Liszt's only concern was with interpretation, sometimes analysing a piece note by note, bar by bar. 'In the Andante of a Weber sonata I learnt more from Liszt in the first four bars than from all my previous teachers', wrote an early pupil, Wilhelm von Lenz. 'He develops the very spirit of music in you', said Amy Fay. 'He doesn't keep nagging at you but leaves you your own conception. Now and then he will make a criticism, or play a passage, and with a few words give you enough to think of all the rest of your life.' He taught Beethoven from notes and tolerated none of the disrespectful liberties that had characterized his

own playing of the great masters in his concert days. Once, when one of his students was struggling with a particularly difficult line in Beethoven's Opus 110, he made everyone in the room try it in turn, observing good-humouredly: 'Ah yes, when once I begin to play the pedagogue I am not to be outdone'.

No essay on Liszt as a teacher would be complete without a mention of some of the great names among his pupils. Carl Tausig was his first and best pupil, a pianist of such prodigious qualities that Liszt himself proclaimed him as his heir. He died at the tragically early age of twenty-nine. His mantle fell on Hans von Bülow, an altogether exceptional artist, and even more celebrated as a conductor than as a pianist, who graduated from Liszt in the 1850s and went to serve Wagner, as did another outstanding Liszt pupil, the conductor Hans Richter. Nikisch, Klindworth and Felix Mottl were other pupils associated with Weimar in the 1870s who were later celebrated conductors.

Nearly every pianist of note before the First World War was the beneficiary of Liszt's teaching or advice: Anton Rubinstein, Weingartner, Lamond, de Pachmann, Moszkowski, Sofie Menter, Mason, Joseffy, Rosenthal, Pohlig, Stavenhagen, da Motta, Sgambati—the list is endless. And composers too: Smetana, Dvořák, d'Indy, MacDowell, César Franck and Grieg, who, if they were not actually pupils, were grateful for his advice and thankful for Liszt's help in getting their music published for the first time. Borodin came to Weimar; Albéniz travelled all the way from Spain to Budapest to see him. Even Tchaikowsky went to Weimar, but found the Abbé to be a little too extravagant with his praise, even as he was over-generous with his time. 'Liszt, the old Jesuit', he wrote, 'speaks in terms of exaggerated praise of every work which is submitted to his inspection. I have just been to hear a new quartet by Sgambati. Liszt sat in the middle of a bevy of aristocratic ladies, and pretended to be delighted with this pupil's work, than which I have never heard anything so destitute of talent. He is at heart a good man, one of the few great artists who has never shown envy, but he is too much of a Jesuit to be frank and sincere.'

Tchaikowsky was not alone in this criticism. The composer Cornelius also despaired at the way his friend indulged his love of flattery

Liszt with a few of his pupils on the steps of the Hofgartnerei

and the advantage taken of him by the numerous hangers-on.

Female admirers would fight to drain the dregs of his wine, to snatch the discarded butt of his cigar [one actually wore a cigar end in her bodice until she died], to pluck a hair from his head. His generosity towards the hordes of worthless pupils who imposed themselves upon him was unbounded, and he would reply at length to more than two thousand letters a year—all quite unnecessary. He was incapable of standing firm against the demands of his admirers, and weakly shrank from giving offence.

Bülow too used to complain that 'In the best pianist's house one could hear the worst playing'. And there was the celebrated occasion when in July 1880 Bülow, taking advantage of the fact that the Master was confined to his room with a sprained foot, descended on Weimar to 'clean out the Augean stables', as he put it. He made many of the pupils play for him. Most of them he knew were making use of Liszt for their own commercial purposes, merely to be able to advertise at home that they were pupils of Liszt. To a certain female of the species, who played the *Mazeppa* study in awful style, he said that her only qualification for performing the piece was that she had the 'soul of a horse'. Afterwards he called the offenders together and gave them a piece of his mind. 'You have no right to pester the Master any more', he lectured them. 'Do not forget that the Master was born as long ago as 1811, or that he is the essence of goodness and gentleness; and do not misuse him in this revolting way. You ladies in particular; most of you, I assure you, are destined for the myrtle rather than the laurel.'

When Liszt learned what had happened he said, 'Yes, as a matter of fact Bülow is quite right. But he is too hard . . . Tell [all these people] just to wait until Bülow has left, and then come back here.'

How Goethe, Liszt's predecessor in Weimar, would have censured him: 'I have no patience with people who cannot control their benevolent impulses', he once said. 'They are like people who cannot contain their urine.'

Right: Two giants that followed him, Anton Rubinstein and (inset) Frederick Lamont (a cartoon by Lindloff)

Chapter 10

A Sad Ending

Weimar had Liszt, and his native Hungary wanted him. In 1867 he had returned to Budapest for the coronation of Francis Joseph. The welcome he had received was typical of the excitement that Liszt was able to generate, as Janka Wohl's description tells:

You must have before your eyes the majestic river —the blue waters of the Danube; the suspension bridge, that striking link which joins Buda to Pesth. You must picture the fortress of Buda and the royal palace with its girdle of gardens; you must see the smiling and picturesque landscape stretching along the right bank facing the long row of palaces on the other side of the river. And, above all, you must see them wreathed in flowers, dressed in their best, bathed in spring sunshine.

Here an immense crowd of eager sightseers was waiting—on stands, in windows, on the roofs, and in flag-bedecked boats—to see the royal procession which was soon to cross the bridge. The Emperor of Austria, after being crowned king of Hungary at the church of St. Matthias, was to go and take the traditional oath on a hillock, formed of a heap of earth collected from all the different states of Hungary, which had been built up opposite the bridge on the left bank of the river.

When the feverish suspense grew intense, the tall figure of a priest, in a long black cassock studded with decorations, was seen to descend the broad white road leading to the Danube, which had been kept clear for the royal procession. As he walked bareheaded, his snow-white hair floated on the breeze, and his features seemed cast in brass. At his appearance a murmur arose, which swelled and deepened as he advanced and was recognized by the people. The name of Liszt flew down the serried ranks from mouth to mouth, swift as a flash of lightning. Soon a hundred thousand men and women were frantically applauding him, wild with the excitement of this whirlwind of voices. The crowd on the other side of the river naturally thought it must be the king, who was being hailed with the spontaneous acclamations of a reconciled people. It was not *the* king, but it was *a* king, to whom were addressed the sympathies of a grateful nation proud of the possession of such a son . . .

The coronation marked the emergence of

Hungary from a lengthy period of political unrest. The new government was keen to rebuild the artistic life of the nation. Liszt was invited to help found a new Academy of Music in Budapest. He accepted the challenge with typical enthusiasm and generosity.

In 1872 Liszt began what he called his '*vie trifurquée*', a life split into three, divided more or less equally between Weimar, Budapest, and Rome. In 1875 the 'Franz Liszt Academy of Music' was opened with Liszt himself acting as director and personally taking the piano class for the first three or four months of every year.

January to April—Budapest: April to July— Weimar: August to December—Rome. A hundred years ago the journeys were long and tiring. Rome to Budapest took more than sixty hours: Budapest to Weimar, sixty hours: Weimar to Rome, another sixty hours. A triangular life, exhausting enough for a man of half his years. The Princess was worried about his detiorating health: 'His Zigeuner life is not suitable for a man of his age; he is wearing himself out; his digestive system is in a bad way; his regime is fatal; every night he has a fever . . .' In 1881 he fell on the stairs in the Hoffgärtnerei, and limped for many weeks. And then his eyesight began to give way, with the development of a cataract in one of his eyes.

And there were financial worries too. He gave generously from his capital and charged nothing for his lessons. Since 1848 he had refused to play the piano for money and his salary as Honorary Kapelmeister at Weimar was a paltry £200 a year. His only income was from his published compositions, and this in turn had almost dried up as his compositions became less and less popular. His later works were savagely attacked by the critics Hanslick and Esser, and fewer and fewer people wanted to hear them. Liszt was a 'Pianist', and people were unwilling to accept that he could be

Liszt at his desk in the Hofgartnerei, Weimar. The only pictures were those of Beethoven

anything else, as he complained in a letter to a pupil:

It seems to me that Mr Litz [sic] is always welcome when he appears at the piano (especially since he has made a profession of the contrary) but it is not permitted him to have anything to do with thinking and writing according to his own fancy . . . for fifteen years, so-called friends, as well as indifferent and ill-disposed people on all sides, sing, enough to split your head, to this unhappy Mr. Litz [sic], who has nothing to do with it: 'Be a pianist, and nothing but that. How is it possible for you *not* to be a pianist?'

And so keenly did he feel this rejection of his music that he actively discouraged performances of it. 'With regard to performances of my works generally, my disposition and inclination are more than ever completely in the negative . . . It seems to me now high time that I should be somewhat forgotten.' And in another letter we find him writing that 'all the best-known French pianists—with the exception of Saint-Saëns—have not ventured to play anything of mine except transcriptions, my own compositions being considered absurd and insupportable.' Yet he had the courage to go on composing in private, as we shall examine in the concluding chapter.

In the meantime, he gave himself to his pupils. Ernest Newman has observed, perhaps a little unkindly, that Liszt in his too liberal attitude to his hangers-on was primarily concerned to foster a legend of open-heartedness about his name, even so far as to acting with a supreme callousness towards his former love, the Countess d'Agoult. The Countess had re-opened the wound with a second edition of her novel *Nelida*, and Liszt knew that she was preparing her diaries and memoires for publication. Accordingly he broadcast loud and wide the famous phrase *pose et mensonges*—'postures and lies'—and as such her memoires were for a long time regarded. And later he gave his approval to that sorry chapter of falsehoods concerning his relations with the Countess in the official biography of his life by Lina Ramann. It was a deliberate and clever device to forestall the judgement of posterity by blackening the Countess's character for veracity, by declaring in advance that she was incapable by nature of telling the truth. The truth, as Liszt knew only too well, was that she had seen very clearly the essential tragedy of his life—the torment of his divided soul.

No, the closing years were not particularly

happy ones. The ever growing circle of his admirers increasingly isolated him from his friends. Many of his closest friends had died and he missed them sorely. In his loneliness, and with no strong woman to drive him, he fell back more and more on narcotics and cigars. His drinking, too, increased and at one period he was consuming a bottle of cognac a day.

But the friendship that perhaps mattered most to him was revived in 1872. The quarrel with Wagner was patched up. Wagner had married Cosima two years previously. They had not informed Liszt, who had learned of the event like everyone else from the newspapers. Cosima was against a reunion, but Wagner wanted his friend and former champion to be at his side for the laying of the foundation stone for his festival theatre in Bayreuth. He swallowed his pride and wrote to Liszt:

My Great and Dear Friend,

Cosima maintains that you would not come even if I were to invite you. We should have to endure that, as we have had to endure so many things! But I cannot forbear to invite you. And what is it I cry to you when I say 'Come'? You came into my life as the greatest man whom I could address as an intimate friend; you gradually went apart from me, perhaps because I had become less close to you than you were to me. In place of you there came to me your deepest newborn being and completed my longing to know you were very close to me. So you live in full beauty before and in me, and we are one beyond the grave itself. You were the first to ennoble me by his love; to a second, higher life am I now wedded in *her*, and can accomplish what I should never have been able to accomplish alone. Thus you could become everything to me, while I could remain so little

98

to you: how immeasurably greater is gain!

If now I say to you 'Come', I thereby say to you 'Come to yourself!' For it is yourself that you will find. Blessings and love to you, whatever decision you may come to!

> Your old friend,
> RICHARD.

Liszt responded with a full heart:

Dear and Noble Friend,

I am too deeply moved by your letter to be able to thank you in words. But from the depths of my heart I hope that every shadow of a circumstance that could hold me fettered may disappear, and that soon we may see each other again. Then shall you see in perfect clearness how inseparable is my soul from *you both*, and how intimately I live again in that 'second' and higher life of yours in which you are able to accomplish what you could never have accomplished alone. Herein is Heaven's pardon for me: God's blessing on you both, and all my love.

Liszt went to Bayreuth for the laying of the foundation stone, and was thereafter a frequent visitor to Villa Wahnfried, where he delighted Wagner with performances of his scores at the piano, or the playing of a Beethoven sonata.

In December 1882 he visited Wagner, who was wintering in Venice. He had a premonition there of his friend's death and composed two strange and haunting pieces, *La Lugubre Gondola I and II*, inspired by the funeral gondolas he saw on the canals. Two months later Wagner was dead. News was brought to Liszt at his desk in Budapest. He did not look up, but was heard to whisper to himself: 'He today, I tomorrow.'

'Tomorrow' for Liszt was another three years off. He continued the exhausting circle of his '*vie trifurquée*'. The major event of these last years was the celebration, in 1886, of his seventy-fifth anniversary. Concerts were arranged all over Europe to mark the occasion. In April he travelled to London for performances of his *St. Elizabeth Oratorio*, then on to Antwerp and Paris for further performances of the Oratorio and of his *Gran Mass*. By mid May he was back in Weimar for a brief rest; then a trip to Luxembourg before going to Bayreuth for the Wagner festival in July.

He journeyed to Bayreuth by train. Two lovers entered the carriage in the cold, early hours of the morning and insisted on opening the window to observe the dawn. Liszt caught a chill; by the time he reached Bayreuth he had a hacking cough and a high fever. Cosima had not invited him to stay at Wahnfried, so he took to his bed in a room at No. 1 Siegfriedstrasse close by. On Friday the 23rd he attended a performance of *Parsifal* and again on Sunday he attended a performance of *Tristan*. He sat slumped in the back of the Wagner family box, with a handkerchief to his mouth to silence his coughs. When the lights went up for the interval he was noticed by someone in the audience and was called forward to receive an ovation. It was to be his last. He returned to his lodgings and to his sickbed.

Cosima was too pre-occupied with the administration of the festival to attend properly to his needs. She brought him his coffee in the morning but for the rest of the day he was left on his own, as everyone was at the theatre. In the evening of the 26th a doctor was called who forbade Liszt his brandy, a stimulant that he needed now more than ever before. The next day he took a sudden turn for the worse and no-one was aware of his plight. Cosima had forbidden all visitors; a group of his pupils hovered in the street outside, not knowing what to do, and Cosima herself was busy arranging a function at Wahnfried. By the Wednesday his condition was so critical that even Cosima was alarmed and summoned another doctor. He diagnosed pneumonia. On the Thursday one of Liszt's most devoted disciples, Lina Schmalhausen, defied Cosima's ban and visited him. She was shocked by what she saw. On the Friday he became delirious and still Cosima continued at the theatre. But on Saturday, warned that her father's end was near, she spent the whole day at his bedside. In the evening he fell into a coma. Shortly before eleven o'clock he was heard to mutter the name 'Tristan', and a few minutes later he was dead.

Liszt's disciples never forgave Cosima for the lack of respect she had shown towards her father. He had not even received extreme unction, and not a single one of the wishes contained in his will were carried out. He was not buried in the habit of the Order of St Francis, nor was there a Requiem Mass, and the benediction over the remains of this Abbé of the Roman church were pronounced by a Lutheran minister. The funeral took place on 3 August—a side-show to a Wagner festival.

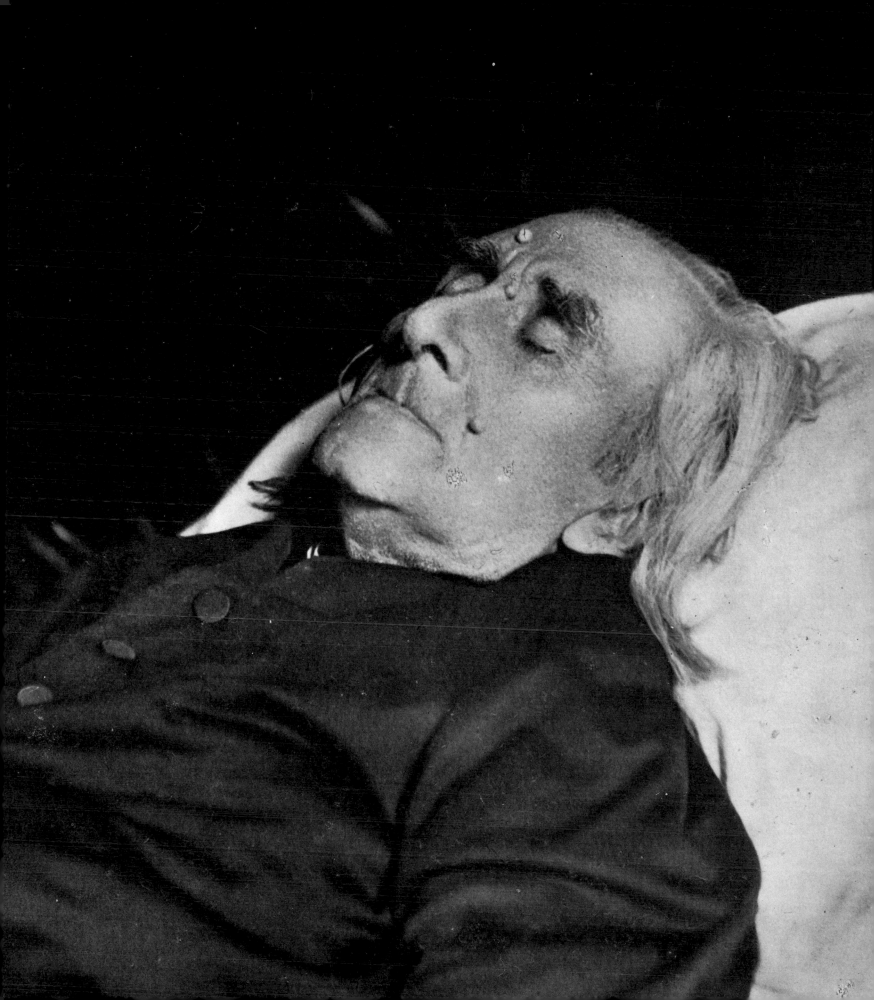

Chapter 11

A Lance Into the Future

Hear what Chopin thought of Liszt as a composer:

When I think of Liszt as a creative artist, he appears before my eyes rouged, on stilts, and blowing into Jericho trumpets *fortissimo* and *pianissimo*—or I see him discoursing on art, on the nature of creativeness and on how one should create. Yet as a creator he is an ass. He knows everything better than anyone. He wants to attain Parnassus on another man's Pegasus. This is *entre nous*—he is an excellent binder who puts other people's works between his covers . . . I still say that he is a clever craftsman without a vestige of talent . . .

England, not unlike Chopin, has been slow to recognize and appreciate Liszt's creative genius. His music is either thought of as being brash and vulgar, 'popular' in the pejorative sense, or as the mere technical bravura displays of the showman. England remembers him first and foremost as the world's greatest pianist, whereas, I fancy, Liszt himself would have preferred to be remembered first and foremost as a composer. 'How is it possible for you *not* to be a pianist?' we seem to say. 'Knowing by experience how little favour my works meet with,' Liszt wrote to Mme Laussot, 'I have been obliged to force upon myself a sort of compulsory disregard of them and a passive resignation.'

Yet even at the times of his greatest discouragement he still continued his restless search for the new. 'The time will yet come when my works are appreciated,' he confided in the last year of his life to a pupil, August Stradal. 'True, it will be late for me because I shall no longer be with you.' And to the Princess Sayn-Wittgenstein he wrote that his aim was 'to hurl a lance as far as possible into the boundless realm of the future.'

Creatively the last fifteen years of his life were devoted almost entirely to finding new forms of expression. We have seen in a previous chapter how he had simplified the earlier versions of his *Paganini Études* and *Transcendental Études*. Many of his later works are plain and almost entirely devoid of showmanship, works such as *Nuages Gris*, *Jadis*, *Die Wiege*, *Via Crucis* and *La Lugubre Gondola I and II*. The expression is direct and simple, and the harmony, with its deliberate vagueness of tonality, shows Liszt to be trying to set music free from the conventions of the past.

Nuages Gris, with its drifting harmonies, leads forward into the realms of 'impressionism'. In 1884 Debussy as a young man heard Liszt in Rome playing some of his recently published pieces. The music made a deep impact on him. *Les Jeux d'Eaux à la Villa d'Este* really paved the way for the French Impressionists. Liszt composed his *Jeux d'Eaux* thirty years before Ravel composed his.

Liszt: *Les Jeux d'Eaux à la Ville d'Este*

Liszt's remarkable *Czárdás Macabre*, written in 1881 though not published until 1951, begins with this startling passage in fifths.

Liszt: *Czárdás Macabre*

Again one thinks of Debussy and the Impressionists. The *Mephisto Waltz* also begins with a highly charged build-up of fifths.

Left: A famous portrait of Liszt by the early photographer Nadar

Previous pages: A painting by Danhauser showing Liszt playing to a group of friends, including Berlioz, Paganini, George Sand and Marie d'Agoult

Liszt: *Mephisto Waltz* No 1

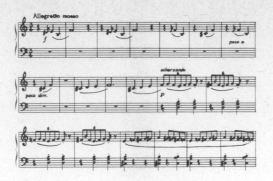

Liszt: *Bagatelle without Tonality*

Dr Alan Walker, in his fascinating essay 'Liszt and the Twentieth Century', shows how Liszt's use of the augmented chord not only led along the path to Impressionism but also paved the way for 'atonality', and how Liszt's experiments in building chords in fourths anticipated Schoenberg by over thirty years.

The *Bagatelle without Tonality*, of 1885, really looks towards the twentieth century.

The first 'official' atonal work is always taken to be Schoenberg's Second String Quartet of 1906. The *Bagatelle*, in its simplicity and directness, reminds us too of Bartok.

Even more remarkable is the keyless opening

Left: Debussy
Below: Schoenberg

Right: photo taken a year before his death, in 1885

theme of the 'Faust' Symphony, written in 1857, which is important for being one of the earliest known twelve-tone rows, anticipating Schoenberg's own discovery of the twelve tone technique of composition by no less than seventy years.

Liszt: 'Faust' symphony, opening theme

Again, Liszt's song *Der Traurige Mönch*, of 1860, is an astonishing piece of work, not only for its use of the whole-tone scale (he himself gave voice to the fear that 'these keyless discords would prove impossible to perform'), but more especially because it is the first example of *sprechgesang*, the words being declaimed not sung, and so laid the foundations for such works as Schoenberg's *Pierrot Lunaire*.

Liszt well and truly hurled his lance into the twentieth century. He wrestled tirelessly with the mysteries of musical creation, knowing full well that his recognition as a composer would not come till after his death. Now, in the light of the developments of almost a century, Liszt's achievements can be seen in their true perspective. He, and not Debussy or Schoenberg, is the father of modern music.

Bartok, after a profound study of Liszt's music, had this to say: 'The great artist's true significance was revealed to me at last. I came to recognize that, for the continued development of musical art, his compositions were more important than either Wagner's or Strauss's.' Constant Lambert is reported to have claimed that Liszt was 'the greatest composer to come out of the nineteenth century', and the Hungarian scholar Szabolcsi has written that 'Liszt threw open the gates of the twentieth century'.

It was for this that Liszt abandoned his career as a virtuoso pianist. His phrase, 'How is it possible for you not to be a pianist?' expresses this central enigma of his life.

Appendix 1

His life in Brief

1811 Franz Liszt (Ferencz List) born October 22 at Raiding. His father, Adam, a land steward on the estates of Prince Esterházy.

1820 Gives first public concert at Sopron, followed by one at Pressburg which leads to a grant to study.

1821 Family moves to Vienna. Franz studies piano with Czerny, and theory with Salieri.

1822 First concert in Vienna, December 1.

1823 Visits Beethoven who later attends Liszt's second Vienna concert and kisses him. Moves to Paris. Studies under Paer after being rejected by Conservatoire.

1824 First visit to England.

1825 Tours provinces of France. Second visit to England. His opera *Don Sanche* performed in Paris.

1826 Tours France and Switzerland.

1827 Third visit to England. Father dies in Boulogne, end of August. Desire to become a priest.

1828 Falls in love with one of his pupils, Caroline de Saint-Cricq.

1829 Continues to teach in Paris. Caroline's mother dies and her father disapproves of their love affair. Nervous collapse. Liszt reported dead and his obituary published in Paris.

1830 July Revolution. Liszt meets Berlioz and hears his *Symphonie fantastique*, 5 December.

1831 Hears Paganini, 9 March—important artistic experience.

1832 Hears Chopin for first time, 26 February.

1834 Liaison with Countess Marie d'Agoult.

1835 Elopement to Switzerland with Countess. Their first daughter, Blandine, born in Geneva, 18 December. Liszt teaches at Geneva Conservatoire.

1836 Holiday in Alps with George Sand and Adolphe Pictet. Returns to Paris in December.

1837 Piano duel with Thalberg. Liszt triumphant. Tours Italy with Countess d'Agoult. Their second daughter, Cosima, born at Como on Christmas Day.

1838 Danube floods. Plays in Vienna on behalf of flood victims.

1839 Long stay in Rome. His son, Daniel, born 9 May. Temporary separation from Countess at end of year. Concerts in Vienna and return to his native Hungary. Start of virtuoso career.

1840–1847 The years of 'Transcendental Execution'. His vast tours as virtuoso: Russia, Germany, Switzerland, France, Rumania, Hungary, England, Scotland, Spain, Portugal, Poland, Denmark, Turkey. Numerous love affairs: Bettina von Arnim, Charlotte Hagn, Lola Montez, Princess Belgiojoso, Caroline Unger, Camille Pleyel, 'La Dame aux Camélias' among them.

1842 Becomes Music Director at Weimar. Holidays with Countess d'Agoult and the children on the island of Nonnenworth in the Rhine.

1844 Parts from the Countess d'Agoult.

1846 Daniel Stern (the Countess d'Agoult) publishes her novel 'Nelida', an account of her relationship with Liszt.

1847 Liaison with Princess Carolyne Sayn-Wittgenstein begins. Gives last concert at Elizabetgrad in Russia. From then on never earns a further penny from playing, conducting or teaching.

1848 Liszt settles in Weimar as Honorary Kappelmeister of the Grand-Ducal Court. The Princess joins him and they live together in the Altenberg.

1849 Liszt conducts *Tannhäuser* at Weimar. Shelters Wagner who is on the run after revolutionary activities in Dresden.

1850 Liszt conducts first performance of Wagner's *Lohengrin*, Weimar August 27th.

1851 Hans von Bülow becomes a pupil.

1852 Berlioz week in Weimar.

1856 Bülow engaged to Cosima.

1857 Bülow marries Cosima.

1858 Liszt resigns from Weimar.

1859 His son Daniel dies, aged twenty.

1860 Princess Sayn-Wittgenstein goes to Rome to arrange their marriage. Liszt writes his testament.

1861 Marriage to Princess postponed on eve of wedding.

1862 Death of his daughter Blandine, aged twenty-seven.

1863 Retreats into semi-religious retirement. Visited by Pope Pius IX at the oratory of the Madonna del Rosario in Rome.

1865 Liszt becomes an Abbé.

1866 Liszt's mother dies in Paris, 6 February.

1867 His triumphant reception in Budapest at the coronation of Franz-Josef. Wagner elopes with his daughter Cosima. Wagner and Liszt quarrel.

1868 Liszt moves to the Villa d'Este.

1869–1886 The '*vie trifurquée*'. Liszt emerges from his religious retirement and begins his life split between Rome, Weimar and Budapest.

1869 Liszt invited back to Weimar by the Grand-Duke, moves into the Hofgärtnerei. For three months in the summer of every year until his death he receives hordes of pupils from all over the world.

1870 Cosima is divorced from Bülow and marries Wagner. The Olga Janina (the Cossack Countess) episode.

1871 Liszt elected a Royal Hungarian councillor.

1872 The breach with Wagner healed. Wagner and Cosima visit him in Weimar. Liszt goes to Bayreuth for the laying of the foundation stone of Wagner's festspielhaus.

1875 The Franz Liszt Academy of Music opens in Budapest. Liszt is the Director, and personally takes the piano classes for the first three months of every year. Liszt attends rehearsals of the *Ring* at Bayreuth.

1876 Deaths of the Countess Marie d'Agoult and George Sand.

1879 Liszt becomes Canon of Albano, now entitled to wear a cassock.

1883 Wagner dies. Liszt conducts memorial concert on Wagner's birthday, 22 May.

1886 Visits London, Antwerp, Paris, Luxembourg for concerts in celebration of his seventy-fifth year. Goes to Bayreuth for Wagner festival. Develops pneumonia. Dies in Bayreuth, 31 July, and is buried there.

1887 Princess Carolyne von Sayn-Wittgenstein dies in March a fortnight after completing the twenty-fourth volume of her 'Causes Intérieures' which occupied her for the final twenty-five years of her life.

Appendix 2

Further Reading

d'Agoult, Comtesse *Mémoires 1838–54* (Paris, 1927)

—*Correspondence de Liszt et de Madame d'Agoult* (Paris, 1933)

—(as Daniel Stern) *Nélida* (Paris 1846)

Apponyi, Count Albert *Memoirs* (London, 1935)

Bache, Constance *Brother Musicians* (London, 1901)

Bartha, Dénes von *Franz Liszt, 1811–1886* (Leipzig, 1936)

Beckett, Walter *Liszt* (Master Musicians Series) (London, 1956)

Bory, Robert *La Vie de Franz Liszt* (Paris, 1937)

Calvocoressi, M. D. *Liszt* (Paris, 1906)

Chantavoine, Jean *Franz Liszt* (Paris, 1950)

Day, Lillian *Paganini of Genoa* (London 1966)

Fay, Amy *Music Study in Germany* (London, 1893; New York, 1965)

Franz, Robert (Olga Janina) *Souvenir d'une Cosaque* (1874–75)

Göllerich, August *Franz Liszt* (Berlin, 1908)

Gregorovius *Roman Journal* (London, 1911)

Habets, A. *Letters of Liszt and Borodin* (ed. Rosa Newmarch, London, 1895)

Hallé, Sir Charles   *Life and Letters* (London, 1896)
Hevesy, André de   *Liszt, ou le roi Lear de la musicque* (Paris, 1936)
Hill, Ralph   *Liszt* (London, 1936)
Hugo, Howard, E. (ed)   *Letters of Franz Liszt to Marie zu Sayn-Wittgenstein* (Harvard, 1963)
Kapp, Julius   *Franz Liszt* (Berlin 1909)
—*Liszt und Wagner* (Berlin, 1909)
La Mara (ed)   9 volumes of letters
Laszlo, Z and Mateka, B   *His Life in Pictures* (London 1968)
Mackenzie, Sir Alexander   *A Musician's Narrative* (London, 1918)
Newman, Ernest   *The Man Liszt* (London, 1934)
Nowak, Leopold   *Franz Liszt* (Vienna, 1936)
Ollivier, Blandine   *Liszt, le musicien passionné* (Paris, 1936)
Ollivier, Daniel   *Autour de Mme d'Agoult et Liszt : Letters* (Paris, 1941)
Philipp, L.   *La Technique de Franz Liszt* 5 vols (Paris, 1932)
Pictet, Adolphe   *Un Voyage à Chamonix*
Pohl, Richard   *Franz Liszt* (Peipzig 1883)
Portalès, Guy de   *La Vie de Franz Liszt* (Paris 1926) (trans. by Brooks, E. S. as *Franz Liszt, the Man of Love.*)
—*Liszt et Chopin* (Paris 1929)
Prod'homme, J. G.   *Franz Liszt* (Paris, 1910)
Raabe, Peter   *Franz Liszt : Leben und Schaffen* 2 vols (Stuttgart, 1931)
Ramann, Lina   *Franz Liszt als Künstler und Mensch* (1880), (1st vol only trans. by Cowdrey, E.) (London, 1882)
Rellstab, Ludwig   *F.Liszt* (1842)
Revue Musicale—special Liszt number (Paris, 1928)
Rostand, Claude   *Liszt* (Paris, 1960)
Sand, George   *Lettres d'un Voyageur*
Searle, Humphrey   *The Music of Liszt* (London, 1954)
—*Liszt*: article in Grove's Dictionary (London, 1954)
Schonberg, Harold   *The Great Pianists* (New York, 1964)
Sitwell, Sacheverell   *Liszt* (London, 1934; revised 1955)
Szabolcsi, Bence   *The Twilight of Liszt* (Budapest, 1956)
Wagner, Cosima   *F, Liszt* (Munich, 1911)
Walker, Alan   *Liszt* (The Great Composer's Series) (London, 1971)
—(ed.)   *Franz Liszt, The Man and His Music—a Symposium* (London, 1970)
Wallace, William   *Liszt, Wagner and the Princess* (London, 1927)
Westerby, Herbert   *Liszt, Composer, and his Piano Works* (London, 1936)
Wohl, Janka   *François Liszt* (Leipzig, 1887)
Zorelli, Sylvia (Olga Janina)   *Les amours d'une Cosaque—par un ami de l'Abbé X*
—*Le Roman de pianiste et de la Cosaque* (1874–5)

Of the books published in English I would especially like to recommend the following short list:

Sacheverell Sitwell: *Liszt* Cassell, 1955.
This remains the only major biography of Liszt in English. It is quite splendid
Humphrey Searle: *The Music of Liszt* Williams & Norgate 1954
An impressive survey of Liszt's music.
Alan Walker (Editor): *Franz Liszt, The Man and His Music* Barrie & Jenkins, 1970.
A symposium with contributions by: Sacheverell Sitwell, David Wilde, John Ogdon, Humphrey Searle, Robert Collet, Louis Kentner, Arthur Hedley, Christopher Headington, and Alan Walker.
This is an excellent collection of essays covering all aspects of Liszt's work. The contributions by experienced performing musicians is especially valuable.
Walter Beckett: *Liszt* (The Master Musicians Series) Dent, 1956
A good shorter study of the man and his music.
Ernest Newman: *The Man Liszt* Cassell, 1934
A fascinating, if rather harsh, character study

Appendix 3

Catalogue of Selected Works

Liszt wrote more than 1300 works. The catalogue that follows lists only the more important of these. Readers who are interested in a more detailed catalogue are advised to consult the excellent, complete catalogue of Liszt's work in the Symposium, edited by Alan Walker: *Franz Liszt, the Man and His Music.* Readers might also be interested in Sacheverell Sitwell's catalogue in his volume, *Liszt,* in which the author has adopted the practice of Baedeker, awarding stars to works that he judges to be of special merit.

A ORIGINAL WORKS

1 PIANO SOLO

1835   *Album d'un Voyageur*
    1 Impressions et Poésies (7 pieces)
    2 Fleurs Mélodiques des Alpes (3)
    3 Paraphrases: Trois Airs Suisses
1855   *Années de Pèlerinage, Première Année: Suisse*
    1 Chapelle de Guillaume Tell
    2 Au lac de Wallenstadt
    3 Pastorale
    4 Au bord d'une source
    5 Orage
    6 Vallée d'Obermann
    7 Églogue
    8 Le Mal du Pays.
    9 Les Cloches de Genève
1858   *Années de Pèlerinage. Deuxième Année: Italie*
    1 Sposalizio
    2 Il Penseroso
    3 Canzonetta di Salvator Rosa
    4 Sonetto 47 del Petrarca
    5 Sonetto 104 del Petrarca
    6 Sonetto 123 del Petrarca
    7 Fantasie, quasi Sonata: d'après une lecture de Dante
    8–10 Venezia e Napoli:
        Gondoliera
        Canzone
        Tarantella
1883   *Années de Pèlerinage. Troidème Année*
    1 Angelus
    2 Cyprès de la Villa d'Este
    3 Cyprès de la Villa d'Este
    4 Les Jeux d'Eaux à la Villa d'Este.
    5 Sunt lacrymae rerum, en mode hongrois
    6 Marche Funèbre
    7 Sursum corda
1885   *Bagatelle sans Tonalité*
1848   *Ballade No 1, in D flat major*
1854   *Ballade No 2, in B minor*
1854   *Berceuse*
1840   *Trois Valses-Caprices*
1850   *Consolations* (six)
1885   *Czárdás obstiné*
    Czárdás macabre
1849   *Études de Concert* No 1 in A flat
                      No 2 in F minor
                      No 3 in D flat

1849–63   *Deux Études de Concert*
    1 Waldesrauschen
    2 Gnomenreigen

1830	*Études en Forme de Douze Exercices pour Piano* (Opus 1)
1854	*Études d'Exécution Transcendante*
	1 Preludio
	2 A minor
	3 Paysage
	4 Mazeppa
	5 Feux Follets
	6 Vision
	7 Eroica
	8 Wilde Jagd
	9 Ricordanza
	10 F minor
	11 Harmonies du Soir
	12 Chasse-Neige
1854	*Étude de Perfectionnement: Ab-Irato*
1841	*Galop in A minor*
1838	*Grand Galop Chromatique*
1853	*Harmonies Poétiques et Religieuse*
	1 Invocation
	2 Ave Maria
	3 Bénédiction de Dieu dans la solitude
	4 Pensée des morts
	5 Pater noster
	6 Hymne de l'enfant à son réveil
	7 Funérailles, October 1849
	8 Miserere d'après Palestrina
	9 Andante lagrimoso
	10 Cantique d'amour
1851–1885	*Hungarian Rhapsodies* (Twenty)
	No 15 is the famous Rákóczy March
1877	*Impromptu in F Sharp*
1866	*Deux Légendes*
	1 St François d'Assise prédicant aux Oiseaux
	2 St François de Paule marchant sur les Flots
1883	*La Lugubre Gondola*
1860	*Mephisto Waltz* No 1
1881	No 2
1883	No 3
1884	*Mephisto Polka*
1881	*Nuages Gris*
1852	*Deux Polonaises*
	1 E major
	2 C minor
1845	*Rhapsodie Espagnole*
1865	*Grand Solo de Concert*
1854	*Sonata in B minor*
1883–5	*Ungarische Bildnisse*
	Seven Hungarian Portraits
1879–86	*Trois Valses Oubliées*
1865	*Via Crucis*
1882	*Weihnachtsbaum*
	The Christmas Tree: collection of twelve pieces

2 PIANO AND ORCHESTRA

1857	*Concerto No 1 in E Flat*
1863	*Concerto No 2 in A Flat*
1864	*Hungarian Fantasia*
1840	*Malédiction* (string orchestra)
1859	*Totentanz*

3 OTHER KEYBOARD WORKS
(a) Two Pianos

1856	*Concerto pathétique*
1865	*Totentanz*

(b) Organ

1852	*Ad Nos ad Salutarem Undam*: Fantasia and Fugue upon the Chorale from Meyerbeer's 'Le Prophete'
1855	*Prelude and Funge on the name B.A.C.H.*

4 ORCHESTRA

1856	*'Dante' Symphony*
1854	*'Faust' Symphony*
1862	*Two Episodes from Lenau's 'Faust'*
	1 Night Ride
	2 Dance in the Village Inn (1st Mephisto-Waltz)

	Symphonic Poems	
1857	1	Ce qu'on entend sur la Montagne
1856	2	Tasso-Lamento e Trionfo
1878		—Epilogue: Triomphe Funèbre de Tasso
1856	3	Les Préludes
1856	4	Orpheus
1850	5	Prometheus
1858	6	Mazeppa
1856	7	Festklänge
1857	8	Héroïde Funèbre
1856	9	Hungaria
1859	10	Hamlet
1856	11	Hunnenschlacht
1859	12	Die Ideale
1883	13	Von der Wiege bis zum Grabe

5 VOCAL WORKS
(a) Opera

1824–5	*Don Sanche* (unpublished)

(b) Choral

1866	*Christus*—an Oratorio
1862	*The Legend of Saint Elizabeth*—an Oratorio
1874	*Die Glocken des Strasburgen Münsters*
1855	*Graner Mass*—for chorus, soloists, and full orchestra
1867	*Hungarian Coronation Mass*
1886	*Missa choralis* in A minor—full chorus and organ
1863	*Psalms*: xiii—Tenor, choir, full orchestra
1871	cxvi—choir and piano
1866	cxxviii—choir and organ

(c) Songs

Liszt wrote nearly seventy songs: these include—
Die Lorelei
Liebesträume
Mignon's Song
Three Sonnets of Petrach

Liszt wrote also several 'Musical Recitations'—
The most celebrated of these is: *Der traurige Mönch*

6 CHAMBER MUSIC

1875–6	*Elegie:*
	1 Cello, piano, harp and harmonium
	2 Cello and piano
	3 Violin and piano
1881	*Romance Oubliée* viola, or violin, or cello and piano
1883	*Am Grabe Richard Wagners* String quartet and harp.

B ARRANGEMENTS

1 OPERATIC TRANSCRIPTIONS FOR PIANO
These include:

1847	Auber: *Tarantelle de Bravura* from *Masaniello*
1840–8	Bellini: *Grande Fantasie sur La Sonnambula*
1841	*Grande Fantasie sur Norma*
1841	Donizetti: *Réminiscences de Lucia di Lammermoor*
1841	*Réminiscences de Lucrezia Borgia*
1868	Gounod: Waltz from *Faust*
1838	Halévy: *Réminiscences de la Juive*
1841	Meyerbeer: *Réminiscences de Robert le Diable*
1841	*Le Prophète*
1841	Mozart: *Don Juan Fantasie*
1843	*Figaro Fantasie*
1836	Pacini: *Fantasie sur le Niobe*
1880	Tchaikowsky: Polonaise from *Eugène Onegin*
1860	Verdi: *Ernani Fantasie*
1859	*Rigoletto*—the quartet
1860	*Trovatore*
1867	*Don Carlos*: Coro di Festa and Marcia funèbre
1883	*Réminiscences de Simone Boccanegra*
1861	Wagner: *Rienzi Fantasie*
1862–73	*The Flying Dutchman*
1849–64	*Tannhäuser*
1853–64	*Lohengrin*
1858	*Tristan and Isolda*
1875	*Rheingold*
1871	*Meistersinger*
1883	*Parsifal*

2 TRANSCRIPTIONS OF SONGS FOR PIANO

1860	Chopin: *Six Chants polonaise*
1860	Liszt: *Six songs*

1 Lorelei
2 Am Rhein
3 Mignon's Song
4 Es war einmal ein König
5 Der du von dem Himmel bist
6 Angiolin da biondo crin

Tre Sonetti di Petraca (see Piano solo)
Glanes de Woronince   1849

1838	Mercadante: *Les Soirées Italiennes*
1860	Mozart: *Ave Verum*
1838	Rossini: *Les Soirées Musicales*
1838–56	Schubert:

Liszt transcribed nearly sixty of Schubert's songs, the
following among them:

Abschied
Auf dem Wasser zu singen
Der Atlas
Der Doppelgänger
Der Jäger
Der Leiermann
Der Lindenbaum
Der Wanderer
Die Forelle
Die junge Nonne
Erlkönig
Frühlingsglaube
Gretchen am Spinnrade
Gute Nacht
Meeresstille
Ständchen

1849–81	Schumann (these include):
	Widmung
	Frühlingsnacht

3 TRANSCRIPTIONS OF INSTRUMENTAL PIECES
Bach, Johann Sebastian:

1839	*Fantasia and Fungue for Organ*, G minor
1839	*Six organ Preludes and Fugues*
1850	*Variations on the Prelude, 'Weinen, Klagen'*
1845–65	Beethoven: All 9 symphonies
1840	*Septet*
1854	Berlioz: *Benvenuto Cellini*
1840	*Faust*
1836–40	*Symphonie Fantastique*
1880	*Harold en Itálie*
1886	César Cui: *Tarantella*
1880	Handel: *Almira, Sarabande and Chaconne*
1856	Mendelssohn: *Midsummer Night's Dream*
	—Wedding March
	—Dance of the Elves
1838	Paganini: *Six Grandes Études d'après les Caprices de Paganini*
1852	(revised)
1846	Rossini: *Overture to William Tell*
1877	Saint-Saëns: *Danse Macabre*
1852	Schubert: *Les Soirées de Vienne*
1846	Weber: Overture, *Der Freischütz*
1854	Overture, *Oberon*

4 ORCHESTRAL ARRANGEMENTS

1886	Liszt: Six of the *Hungarian Rhapsodies*
1861	*March Funèbre*, from *Années de Pèlerinage*, Book Three
1859–71	Schubert: *Four Marches*
1881	Zarembski: *Deux Danses Galiciennes*

C LITERARY WORKS OF LISZT

1852	*Frédéric Chopin*
1859	*Die Zigeuner und ihre Musik in Ungarn*

(Eng. trans. 1926 by Edwin Evans Sr, as *The Gipsy in Music*)

1859	*Uber Fields Nocturnen*

These are Liszt's main literary works. However he contributed
many articles and essays to numerous musical journals and these
have been published in six volumes. His essays on Berlioz and
Wagner did much to establish these composers.

Liszt also edited the works of other composers; Chopin's *Études*,
Field's *Nocturnes*, Bach's *Chromatic Fantasy*, Beethoven's Piano
Quartets, various Schubert Sonatas, among others.

The publishers would like to thank the following contributors for the use of
their material:

Kunst Archiv 6, 8, 9, 12b, 12l, 14, 15, 16, 19r, 20, 22t, 25, 27l, 33, 38, 48,
52, 53, 55, 56, 57, 61, 62, 67, 70, 71, 72, 73, 77, 79, 80, 84b, 89, 90, 91, 93,
94, 96, 97t and b, 98, 101, 102/3
Liszt Museum, Weimar 7t and b
Mansell Collection 11t, 11b, 12r, 17, 18, 22b, 24, 26, 27, 34, 36, 40, 45, 49,
50, 54, 58/9, 64, 65, 68, 74t, 74b, 82, 84, 86, 88, 93, 104, 106
München Städt. Galerie des Lenbach-Haus 78
Schloss Nymphenburg, Munich (Blauer) 63
Spectrum Colour Library 42/3
All other material is the property of the publishers

Index